D0982448

The Hungry and Sick

"The Family"—father Luigi, me Stanley, mother Flavia, sister Maria.

The Hungry and Sick

Notes on My 196
Days in the E.T.O.

Stanley W. Raffa

VANTAGE PRESS
New York

Excerpts in Chapter IX reprinted from the
Shreveport (LA) Times (now defunct).

FIRST EDITION

Copyright © 2005 by Stanley W. Raffa

Published by Vantage Press, Inc.
419 Park Ave. South, New York, NY 10016

Manufactured in the United States of America
ISBN: 0-533-15071-X

Library of Congress Catalog Card No.: 2004097652

0 9 8 7 6 5 4 3 2 1

Contents

Author's Note

This story is true. It occurred sixty years ago and was written right after it happened. The basic story took about two weeks to write, about the time it took to cross the Atlantic on a convoy. It has undergone revision from time to time, but it is essentially as it was originally written. Recently, I have put some work into it just to get it in shape for the sixtieth anniversary of our capture.

The title, *The Hungry and Sick,* is a play on words on the 106th Division to which I was assigned; heavy weapons machine gunner, Pfc., Company D, 1st Battalion, 422nd Regiment. My dog tag was #42054532. This was the ill-fated division that lost over 8,500 men during the "Battle of the Bulge." Over 7,000 men were captured. This is what happened to some of them.

As I note in the last chapter, I do not think that our experiences as prisoners of war (POWs) were unique. But I think that it was worth keeping track of.

Stanley W. Raffa
May, 1945

The Hungry and Sick

I

On the *Aquitania*

In the great war to end all wars (the second one, that is), overseas service officially began the day a soldier left the continental limits of the United States. This story begins that day, October 21, 1944.

We left Pier 92 in New York City at 8:00 A.M., and by 8:20, our ship, the *Aquitania,* was steaming past the Statue of Liberty. For security reasons, we were told, we were not allowed on the open decks to bid her farewell. But some of us managed to get one last glimpse of the "Old Lady" as we passed by her, and while our true emotions may have been masked by the stoic expressions of soldiers, they were, nevertheless, in the glorious tradition, and we knew that it would probably be some time before we would be seeing her again. For whatever significance she may hold for the immigrant approaching our shores, with all the hope she may hold for a new life, the departing native holds her in reverence as the symbol of all he leaves behind: family, friends, and a way of life. And during those moments we were all of a similar thought.

But wisely, the soldier's mind does not permit his thoughts to linger too long with the nostalgia of the past, and no sooner had we lost sight of the torch when we became preoccupied with the immediacy of the present and anticipation of the future. We were 9,000 strong aboard the *Aquitania,* the second contingent of the 106th Division, headed for England. (The first contingent used the *Queen Elizabeth.*)

For me, the trip held great expectations. Though a native New Yorker, just barely nineteen, I was hardly the picture of worldliness. I was born on the Upper East Side. My parents, immigrants to this country from Italy (my father, already a citizen by virtue of World War I) had always worked hard to provide the best in the way of necessities. My father was a furniture varnisher, my mother embroidered at home until my younger sister, nearly eleven, was old enough to go to school by herself, after which, my mother worked as a seamstress in a dress house. We had no car, and the only transportation I knew was the "elevated," the subway, the trolly and the ferry. In fact, prior to the service, I had never wandered further south than Staten Island, further west than Englewood, New Jersey, further north than Bear Mountain, New York, and further east than the Rockaways, New York.—We had no car!

I had completed high school and was working six months in an essential industry (draftsman) when I was drafted, officially on November 17, actually on December 8, 1943. (It was a Catholic feast day, the Feast of the Immaculate Conception, which doubled the reason why my mother went to church that morning.) We were to "muster" at the ungodly hour of 5:30 A.M. I made no effort at deferment. My reasons were both patriotic and selfish. I felt it was my duty to go, and most of my friends were already in the service. More than that, it presented me with an opportunity to travel, see new places, and do new things. I had already passed examinations that would enable me to attend college in an accelerated program, which would gain me an engineering degree in three years with a commission waiting for me after graduation (the Army Specialized Training Program, or ASTP). Of course, I never got there. I had already completed ten weeks of basic training (a prerequisite for the college program) when the anticipated invasion of Europe wiped out the program and I found myself a member of the 106th Infantry Division.

I was assigned to D Company, 1st Battalion, 422nd Regiment. "D" was a heavy weapons company consisting of three platoons, two machine gun and one mortar. I was in the second platoon, machine gun. Starting as an ammunition bearer, I worked myself up to a second gunner, then first gunner, which earned me a PFC stripe. The division was located in Camp Atterbury, Indiana, when we joined it from Fort Benning, Georgia. We trained there for some six months, during which time many of the original cadre of the division were shipped overseas as replacement personnel.

For a while, it appeared that the 106th Division was destined to be a paper division relegated to provide trained men as replacements only. Many of us were eighteen and regulations at that time, surprisingly, were such that anyone not nineteen years of age would not be shipped overseas. Eventually, however, a certain stability was attained and the division was allowed to train as a unit without the threat of periodic raids.

About a month before the division received orders to leave Camp Atterbury, there was much speculation as to where we were going or whether we were leaving at all. In June, we received notice that the entire division would participate in a series of maneuvers in Louisiana in September. The division had participated in Tennessee maneuvers prior to its arrival at Atterbury; however, since many of the old cadre had gone by way of the "banana boat" and the division had undergone drastic changes in personnel, this prospect appeared very logical. We soon learned, however, that the maneuvers had been called off. We knew then that it wouldn't be long before we were to go overseas.

Speculation at first had us moving to the Pacific theater of operations until someone cynically remarked that General MacArthur had already refused the 106th Division as well as any other unit that had trained under the Second Army Command. Rumor then had it that the entire Second Army was headed for the European theater of operations. This turned out to be a fairly good rumor, in view of the fact that most of the Second Army eventually did go to Europe although it never fought as a unit. Some of us were of the opinion that we were going to Alaska or Iceland, but there was never to be any talk of snowshoes in the supply room, and we quickly gave that up.

The only people who seemed to know where we were going besides the High Command were the local citizens who insisted that we were going to Europe, and when we finally arrived at Camp Miles Standish Port of Embarcation (in Massachusetts) we knew that they were right and that we were going to England. We were equally certain that we were going to stay in England too, at least until the war was over, after which we would probably take up occupational duties somewhere in Germany. It was inconceivable to us that we might be considered a combat outfit.

We were not to leave from Boston, however. We left Camp Miles Standish by train on October 20, were ferried to Hoboken, New Jersey, to Pier 92 in New York City, and boarded the *Aquitania* that very night. The next morning we were on our way.

It is an old army tradition that soldiers are never happy unless they are complaining. If this were true, then the *Aquitania* carried 8,000 of the happiest soldiers in the U.S. Army that trip. An aging luxury liner in peacetime, it had served as an army transport during the First World War. Pressed into service again, it had already made several trips across the Atlantic without mishap. Its conversion from luxury liner to troopship, however, had wiped out all vestige of luxury, and to most of us, the *Aquitania* was more than an old British tub which gave us the dubious pleasure of cursing her from stem to stern.

Most of our company was quartered on E deck, which was just above water level. The hold was so crowded that whatever little air managed to seep in wasn't quite enough to satisfy the half of us. This condition was tolerable during the day, when we were allowed on the open deck, but at night it was stifling. Since ours was the last deck above sea level, it was also the last deck to provide latrines. Serving as they did our own deck and two more below, these facilities were grossly inadequate.

We received our first meal aboard ship at about ten that morning. Most of us ate it, but by suppertime there were very few of us left who were interested in food. Seasickness was prevalent, and the menu provided little encouragement. Our latrines became overtaxed, and in many cases, those that were two decks below us never quite succeeded in relieving their comfort in private misery. These poor souls, and the many others that rushed up the stairs from the decks below, were greeted with a stomach-wrenching "Yuuuulp!" from the few of us who had managed to retain our gastric balance. The "latrine dashers" became fewer by nightfall, but some were to suffer the entire trip.

Breakfast was attended by less than half the ship the next morning. The meal consisted of lumpy oatmeal and boiled wieners. This unpalatable dish was greeted with all sorts of derisive remarks that need not be quoted here. Needless to say, these comments were so descriptive as to drive anyone trying to make the most of the meal out of the mess hall. The chain of epitaphs was interrupted only when someone rose to leave hurriedly, at which time the entire mess hall urged him to a swifter pace with a deafening "Yuuuulp!"

We had become accustomed to a variety of food at Camp Atterbury. Our own company cooks prepared excellent meals within the limitations of their monthly allowance. Most of the division had spent so much time on maneuvers, bivouacs, and hikes that we came to call ourselves "the bag lunch division." Yet, there is no doubt that the food served on the *Aquitania* was the worst that we had encountered until then. We were fed two meals a day, breakfast and supper.

This arrangement might have been quite adequate since it was quite a job to feed 8,000 men even twice a day. However, twice a day the food was half as much and twice as bad as any we had ever tasted. Breakfast usually consisted of lumpy oatmeal, two soft-boiled eggs, a slice of bread and an apple. Sometimes, half-boiled wieners replaced the eggs. For supper we were satisfied to get a watery stew, but more often it was cold cuts.

With those of us that were eating were half-starved, and those that weren't were even worse off. It was little wonder that many resorted to the black market which the British cooks were running at fifty cents for a man-sized sandwich. When the PX aboard was finally opened, it was sold out the first day, and for two days we ate nothing but crackers. This prompted the British to complain that their food was going to waste.

We had our first abandon-ship drill the second morning. It took us over twenty minutes to clear the holds and take our positions on the open decks. Eventually, we narrowed the time down to six minutes, thereby breaking some sort of record. At first it was boring just standing on deck waiting for the drill to end, but soon we devised a game that provided several hearty laughs. The idea was to trap someone, preferably a noncommissioned officer, to a large tight circle and toss him from side to side until he worked himself out of it. We passed most of our boat drills in this manner and sergeants and privates alike took a beating in the ring. We looked forward to this every morning and probably was the impetus for breaking the record.

That morning, Bob Walker and I took our first walk aboard ship. Bob was jeep driver for our platoon. He had enlisted while he was still seventeen, had completed a semester in the ill-fated Army Specialized Training Program at Indiana University and had undergone basic training at Fort Benning, Georgia, though we were in different regiments at the time. When the ASTP was suddenly dissolved, a thousand men from each regiment were assigned to the 87th Division while the remainder were assigned to the 106th. Since the assignments were made in alphabetical order, we were assigned to the 106th Division and found ourselves in the same squad. We were good friends at Atterbury but really knew little about each other until a few weeks before we left Miles Standish. On free weekends Bob went home to Cincinnati and in Indianapolis we pursued different interests.

The *Aquitania* provided little interest. Any glamour that this sturdy ship may have possessed at one time had been removed in the conversion of a liner to troopship. Looking at the *Aquitania,* it was difficult to realize that she had ever been a luxury liner at all. A sister ship of the *Lusitania,* sunk in World War I, and the *Moritania,* it had survived two World Wars and crossed the Atlantic many times, always without convoy protection. With this record behind it, and with our own propaganda so thoroughly convincing that there were few, if any, German submarines left lurking in the Atlantic; there were very few of us that even thought about possible dangers. The *Aquitania* had taken the northern route, zig-zagging its way toward Ireland, and then to Scotland. This maneuvering, we were told, would fool the Germans, and the ship's speed, greater than their submarines, provided further assurance of safe passage. It was inconceivable that the Germans were unaware of this trip and they were really unable to attempt to impede it. However, the voyage was completely uneventful, which led someone to quip that the Nazis were indeed looking forward to our arrival.

There was very little planned activity aboard ship. There were, of course, the usual card and crap games for those who had money. Since Bob and I were virtually broke, we played hearts or 500 rummy for points. When not playing cards, we passed the hours reading pocket books which we received in a Red Cross gift bag. One book, *Ellery Queen's Chinese Mystery*, held me so entranced that I actually refused to play cards until I had completed it.

On the third evening, it was announced that there would be a movie in the mess hall, an event for which we interrupted a game of hearts to attend. The movie was a good one and an obvious morale booster. It was *Babes on Broadway*, starring Mickey Rooney and Judy Garland. Besides several nostalgic scenes of the Great White Way, it contained a highly propagandistic sequence in which Judy sang a song dedicated to British stiff upper lip, encouraging the legendary Britisher to "Carry on, Johnny Atkins, be a stout fella! Chin up! Cheerio! Carry on!" As corny as it may sound today, the sequence had the desired impact and the entire movie was received with much enthusiasm.

Another intended morale booster was the USO show that was traveling with us to England to entertain the troops. The show was headed by Miss Irene Manning of the stage and screen and was supported by some lesser artists. The troupe put on a show the fourth and fifth evenings in the mess hall, which, unfortunately, was not very enthusiastically received.

The next morning, Miss Manning was seen walking on the upper deck with an Air Force lieutenant. Many of us were milling on the deck below in anticipation of the abandon-ship drill. In our group was Zimand, a little Jewish fellow from Brooklyn, New York, and Larry Williams, a tall, happy-go-lucky fellow from Mississippi. The physical counterparts of Mutt and Jeff, "Zeke" and "Willy" were ever present to promote a situation. On this occasion, they promoted cheers for Miss Manning. But as the chanting of "we want Irene" swelled across the decks, the cry of "we want Urine" was also added. Soon, half the ship was chanting "Irene," and the other half, "urine." It is to Miss Manning's credit, as well as to the credit of all USO performers who had to put up with this kind of shenanigans, that she never gave the slightest awareness of the situation. This placed her in high esteem and the cheers for Miss Manning became loud and sincere.

With the exception of the movies and the USO show, there was very little else in the way of entertainment aboard the *Aquitania*. Boxing and wrestling matches were held on the upper decks, weather permitting, and whenever a GI got the better of a "limey," there were roars of enthusiasm.

The seven days aboard the *Aquitania* passed rather quickly for most of us, and despite some discomforts, almost pleasantly. Our own company had been spared most menial tasks that are a normal part of army life. Once I volunteered to help sweep the mess hall in the hope that I would get some extra food from the kitchen. All but unboiled wieners had been locked up, however. We were offered some hot cocoa, but when we noticed four roaches floating in the vat, we decided to do without it.

The entire trip across the Atlantic was uneventful; even the weather was, for the most part, good. It was unusually warm for late October and except for two rainy days it was pleasant enough to walk the open deck with just a field jacket. The day before we sighted land, we were met by two naval cruisers, which served as escorts for the remainder of the trip. The next afternoon, we caught our first glimpse of the Irish coastline, green and hilly. Even the ocean took on a darker shade of green as we approached the Emerald Isle. We slid up the coast and around Northern Ireland. The next evening we dropped anchor in the Firth of Forth at Greenock, Scotland. Smoking was permitted on the open decks at night for the first time. We stood on the decks and watched the sun disappear behind the Scottish hills while a few tiny lights began to speckle in the town along the coast. It was our last night aboard the *Aquitania*.

II

A Cast of Characters

We disembarked from the *Aquitania* the next morning soon after breakfast. An old ferry took us from the ship to the mainland, after which we boarded a train which was to take us to "somewhere in England." Bob and I managed to find a seat opposite Sandviet, transportation corporal of the motor platoon and Earl Williams, also a driver, not to be confused with Larry, Zeke's pal. By noon, we were on our way.

My first impressions of this new country were good. Scotland can boast of some of the most beautiful scenery ever bestowed a country by nature. It looks much like our midwest with its beautiful green hills and lazy rolling meadows. Scotland, however, like its more conspicuous product, has mellowed with age, and nature has achieved results that seldom appear on picture postcards.

Next to the landscape, it was the British Railway System that impressed me the most. I recall that when the train began to move out of the station, there was no sudden jerk like that usually accompanying the movement of the New York Central, the Pennsylvania, and especially, the Southern Railway Systems. Instead of being catapulted out of our seats as we expected, we hardly noticed the train getting underway. The seats themselves were fairly comfortable, though I must admit that the Jeffersonian and the more modern coaches of the Pennsylvania and the New York Central surpass anything I saw in Britain. This particular train was unlike the conventional British train in which each car was divided into several compartments. Rather, it looked like the old American coaches of the late nineteenth century in which each car was divided into two sections.

These cars, however, had not been allowed to deteriorate with age. Instead, it was noticeable that great care had been taken to keep them available for any emergency. Furthermore, the train moved slowly, made little noise (possibly the tracks were tighter, as may have been the car's construction) and what was even more gratifying, an almost negligible amount of soot crept in through the windows.

We spent that afternoon playing cards, and by nightfall we were in England. Through what towns and cities we passed, I don't know, partially because of the blackout and partially because of my "worldly" ignorance. I recall passing one station where I caught the name "Bovril." Sometime later, we passed another bearing the same name. It struck me that Bovril must be a fairly large place, a county perhaps. It wasn't until I saw Bovril at a third station and I remarked about it that I was informed that it wasn't a place at all, but a health drink. The name Bovril, in capital, gold-crested letters and nothing else to advertise it, certainly had me fooled.

That evening the train stopped at two small stations at which we were given some hot tea at one and a bag lunch apiece at the other. We expected no better than a bag lunch, since our division had been raised on a diet of bag lunches, but it was appreciated, as was the tea. By eleven-thirty, just as I was ready to drop off to sleep, we were told to gather our equipment and prepare to get off the train, as we were nearing our destination.

At about twelve-fifteen the train assumed a creeping pace and finally stopped. We arrived at Fairford, England, a small town some forty miles from Oxford, situated in what was supposed to be the prettiest English countryside. After assembling outside the station, we marched down the country road leading into town. As we marched up the narrow winding streets, we saw no sign of activity, neither outside nor inside the houses, the outlines of which were brought out by the bright glow of a nearly full moon. After a short hike, we arrived at the gates of a park which had once been the estate of a certain Colonel Palmer. Quonset huts now dotted the park, hidden from the air by the autumn foliage of age old trees. Each company was assigned a series of barracks, and our platoon was assigned two, one to each section.

Our hut was cold and barren. Apparently no one had lived there for some time. There was electricity but no lights. There were bedposts and springs, but they were dismembered. Finally, we decided to take some mattresses, lay them on the floor, and get some sleep. It was well past three when I finally closed my eyes.

I woke up at ten that morning to find that a few of the boys had already gone to breakfast. The cooks worked all night fixing the kitchen and preparing the meal. Hugh Griffin, who was our platoon sergeant and an early riser, was just returning from the kitchen. He offered that there was some oatmeal and coffee but no bread and no sugar, and that there wouldn't be any for a few days yet. Bob and I decided to skip breakfast and fix up our bunks instead. We had barely finished assembling them when a call came for two KPs from our platoon. Bob was one of them, and I was left to complete the job.

Details, however, were coming in one after the other, and within a few minutes, almost everyone was chosen to do some dirty work. There were just a few of us left to fix up the hut which was a job in itself. There was a door to be set back on its hinges, the chimney to be fixed, the beds to be assembled, and light bulbs to be stolen from the other huts. When we finally completed the job, the hut began to take on the semblance of fairly good living quarters.

At this point, I would like to acquaint the reader with the men of the Second Section, those of us that made that particular hut our home. I shall start from top rank down, moving from the third to the fourth squads.

The highest ranking N.C.O. in our hut was T/Sgt. Hugh Griffin, our platoon sergeant. He had moved in with the Second Section not only because he favored the section but also because he believed there was more room in our hut. (The First Section had to accommodate the Company Headquarters Section which

I surmised he had little use for.) I admired Sergeant Griffin enormously, and I think most of the platoon did too. He had been in the army since 1939 and rose to the rank of first sergeant from which he was later busted. Soon after, he was given S/Sgt. stripes and became one of the original cadre when he was transferred from the Eightieth Division. He became acting first sergeant twice again but actually never received his stripes because either he messed up the works or was more valuable as a platoon sergeant, where he seemed to feel more at ease anyway. On Tennessee maneuvers, he received his tech sergeant (T/Sgt.) stripes.

Griffin had a manner about him that was almost comical. He had a way of barking orders that was incomparable to any I have ever heard. He could issue a command so fast, accentuating certain parts of it in such a manner as though he was just moving his mouth, uttering loud syllables that only he was able to comprehend. He was the closest thing to a sideshow barker that I had ever known in the army, and together with his flim-flam manner, I often had all I could do to keep from laughing. Thus, he was nicknamed "The Voice," and many were the laughs we had over Griffin's bark.

Another characteristic of T/Sgt. Griffin was his left hand, which had only three fingers, his index and middle fingers having been blown off when a boobytrap exploded in his hand while in the Eightieth Division. This was certainly nothing to laugh about, but we found some humor even in that. Whenever Griffin was deep in thought, he would rub his chin with his three fingers, and as a result, another nickname was pinned to him, that of "Three-Finger Harry." It was nothing novel, but on Griffin it was funny.

Griffin was not a very learned man in so far as education was concerned. It is possible that he never completed high school. Yet, there was something very intelligent about the man. At any rate, he was a good soldier who knew a great deal about tactics. He was also a good faker, and whenever he was in a tight spot with one of the officers, he would always manage to squirm and twist his way out of it. If he got stuck, he'd merely stumble and juggle his words in such a way that the officer, despite his not being able to quite make out what it was that he was talking about, was led to believe that Sergeant Griffin was trying to bring out a point, and Griffin, having five years of army experience to his credit, was usually dismissed without further questioning. Sometimes Griffin would make absurd allegories between two entirely different situations and usually the officer would not contradict him, afraid to admit that Griffin was right (though he couldn't understand his point) and likewise afraid to say he was wrong because he might just be right.

I liked Sgt. Griffin, and I think he liked me. I don't say he was partial. Griffin liked most anyone who didn't try to be a wise guy or take advantage of him when his back was turned. He liked his rank, and sometimes he liked to force it down somebody's throat (usually a noncom's, for they represented the greatest challenge to his rank), just to show him that he was still boss. For this reason, he made several enemies, and some of the older men in the company claimed that he was a louse during basic training. At times, when Griffin felt he had become too lenient with the platoon, he would fly into a rage and threaten all sorts of things at individuals or the platoon as a whole, but most of these threats were never fulfilled.

Staff Sergeant (S/Sgt.) Don Photenhauer was our section sergeant and next in line for Griffin's job (or so it appeared) in case of any eventuality. Photenhauer had been with the 106th since inauguration. He had gone through basic training at Fort Jackson and maneuvers in Tennessee. He was attending the University of Michigan when his "greetings" arrived and had played college football with the varsity team. He was a sturdy fellow, intelligent as well as athletic. Generally, he was a good egg, though he too had his faults. His main one was that he insisted on being obeyed almost without question, and the less excuses the better. He also insisted that he was always right and disliked anyone to tell him otherwise, unless it was someone with a higher rank from his. At Atterbury, we always considered

S/Sgt. Photenhaur as the ideal section sergeant to have under fire. He was rugged and probably knew the machine gun better than anyone else in the platoon.

Buck Sergeant Saunders was squad leader of the Third Squad. He too had been with the 106th Division since its beginnings. He had been squad leader once before, had served in the capacity of instrument corporal in the supply room, and had been appointed squad leader again when a mass POE (Port of Embarkation) roundup in Atterbury disseminated half the platoon. He was a quiet fellow, a native of Alabama. He was intelligent (a college man), well-to-do, and a little sensitive, as well as self-conscious, about himself. He was timid in picking his men for details mainly because he didn't like to do it, and he was equally timid in fighting for his squad when there was a break coming. He and Photenhaur were good friends.

Saunders's first gunner was Private First Class (PFC) Nelson Charron, a young fellow from Chatham, New York. Charron, along with others, had been assigned to the outfit in June after being turned down for POE at Fort Meade for being under the age limit. Having had basic training with a heavy weapons company in Camp Blanding, Florida, he was almost immediately appointed first gunner.

Charron was an easy-going fellow who worked hard when he had to but never overdid it when it wasn't necessary. He was conscientious, and though he knew his machine gun pretty well, he never tried to outshine the next person. While, for a time, his squad was minus a squad leader, he took charge of it and worked very hard, expecting, perhaps, to be given the position permanently. Saunders took over, however, and Charron reverted back to first gunner. Though he was probably better off without the responsibilities that went with the job, Charron, with all due respect, should have received the stripes.

John Durbin was second gunner in Saunders's squad. He and Charron were an excellent team, and up until "the Bulge," they were inseparable. It struck me that he and Charron were the best gunner team in the company.

Durbin was from Pittsburgh, Swissvale area, and had been in the service for a shorter length of time than any of us. He had been drafted in late March of 1944 and joined the 106th late in July, straight from basic training. He knew his machine gun fairly well and was appointed second gunner almost as soon as he joined the company.

The rest of the squad consisted of PFC Bernard J. Vogel, PFC Ridgely, and Pvt. Morris. BJ meant well but he talked too much. That was one reason why he didn't remain first gunner too long after Charron came along. The other was that he spent too much time in the hospital at Atterbury through no fault of his own. Vogel hailed from Brooklyn, New York, and his family were good friends of the Zimanda. He, like so many of us, had come up from ASTP-Benning where he was in the Fifteenth Regiment.

Ridgely was a small, quiet fellow who didn't talk much and always did what he was told without much mitigation and was therefore especially liked by everyone. Morris was exactly the opposite. He too was a small fellow, but he claimed that he had some Indian blood in him which, he said, accounted for his being a little wild. There were times when you could get along with Morris, but mostly you couldn't with any satisfying results. He was especially repulsive when he was drunk and was among the least liked in the platoon.

Driving for the Third Squad was PFC Carl E. Grube. He was a tall, quiet fellow from Dover, New Jersey, and had been with the outfit since maneuvers. Due to an accident, he was forced to walk around with a slight limp (though many swore he lost it when he was out on pass). Through their association in the motor pool, Carl and Bob were good friends.

Turning to the Fourth Squad, our squad, we had Sgt. Paul Grizzle of Calhoun, Georgia, who was squad leader. Grizzle had the strength of an ox, but was one of the nicest men in the company. He was the proverbial take-the-shirt-off-his-back person to help you. He hadn't gotten very far in school down in Georgia, but he had a sharp analytical mind, and when it came to explaining the more complicated intricacies of the machine gun, Grizzle knew what he was talking about. The one thing we kidded him most about was his deep Southern drawl and his slow, deliberate manner of speech. Many a time we had to tell him to get the marbles out of his mouth, and Grizzle took the joke in the same spirit in which it was given.

I was first gunner for the fourth squad. I had served as ammo bearer in one squad, then second gunner in the Fourth Squad, and in July, when the first gunner left for the paratroops, I was given the job, mostly, I think, because either Griffin or Photenhaur saw that, if nothing else, I usually did my work. I considered myself as knowing the machine gun fairly well, as I could disassemble and assemble it blindfolded and with considerable ease.

Our second gunner was James Monroe. Monroe had had his ups and downs in D Company. He too had been with the 106th since its innaugural at Fort Jackson, South Carolina. He had been first gunner several times and was made squad leader during maneuvers. He never held that job long enough, however, to obtain his stripes. He was caught in town, one night during Tennessee maneuvers, having left his machine gun, fully stripped, to rust in the rain. Later, he went AWOL for a week, was demoted to second gunner for the Second Squad and finally ended up as second gunner for the Fourth Squad when he and the first gunner (Brummer) were getting along too well (especially where Scotch was concerned). Each had been busted and promoted so many times from PFC to Pvt. and back again that they were vying for honors as to who held the record.

I couldn't quite understand Monroe sometimes. We got along fairly well together, though not as two gunners should. I always tried to be good friends with him, but we were two different types of individuals entirely, and somehow a barrier always seemed to stand between us. Monroe was a very independent fellow and as stubborn as a Missouri mule, which is where he hailed from. He was a farmer, as one could easily tell by talking to him, and so we nicknamed him "Lum." We used to enjoy calling him that, and he didn't seem to mind. I believe that Lum resented being second gunner. He seemed to know more about the machine gun than I did, and he had been with the company a lot longer.

One thing we all admired about Monroe was his ingenuity and his ability to improvise. He built us a washing machine from two tin cans and which worked wonders. And as a I recall it, he was the one who stole the first light bulbs for us in Palmer Park. Whenever there was something to fix, someone would suggest that Lum fix it, and he was more than willing to do it. He was also one of our foremost hillbilly singers and seemed to know more country songs than Roy Acuff had in his repertoire.

The next man in our squad probably should never have been in the army at all. I shall refer to him simply as JT.

JT had been in the U.S. Army for approximately eight years, during which time he had been court-martialed (by his own admission) six or eight times. I first met JT the very first night I was assigned to the company. He was drunk and asked me to lend him five dollars, which I didn't have anyway. The next night, he was drinking a bottle of West Point hair tonic with a fellow crony of his. The third night, he was burning some shoe polish hoping to extract whatever alcohol he could from it. He was in a joking mood this time, but it struck me that this guy was something of a character. I found out more about him as time went on and learned that he had been in Panama, where he apparently had tried to drink the place dry of its rum.

That was in April. In May, JT was given a furlough, which, he said, was only his second during his entire army career. "Now. I ask you," he sneered one day, "is that fair?" He couldn't understand, neither did he bother to explain, that he had gone AWOL so often and had been in trouble so many times that he was lucky to get this one. So this time, in order to make up for all the legal days he had lost, he decided to overstay his furlough a month, and would have remained longer had he not been caught. He explained this time that he had just married and that his grandmother had died. Now that he had a wife, he said, he would be a changed man. But Captain Porter was taking no chances. JT was court-martialed again and was put in the stockade for four months.

This proved to be the best break JT was ever to receive in the army. Every day except Sunday he was taken out in custody of an armed guard from eight A.M. until six P.M. As the guard was appointed from the company, the restrictions on him meant virtually nothing. During these hours he was supposed to work either in the kitchen or the supply room or march out to the field with the rest of the company. The latter, JT rarely did. He would always have an appointment to go to sick call for either his teeth, his leg, or some other part of his anatomy.

In the kitchen, he would spend most of his time eating, writing to his wife, or telling anecdotes about his lusty days in Panama. In the supply room, he did virtually nothing but get in the way. In short, both the mess sergeant and the supply sergeant, knowing that it was useless to try and put JT to work, preferred not to have him at all. So JT would spend his time in the service club. Instead of the guard leading JT around, it got so that JT was leading the guard around. Sometimes, when one of his crony pals guarded him, he managed to get to town to spend the afternoon with his wife. He told me this himself one day when I was detailed to "guard" him. He claimed that one of the officers knew about it all the time. He would usually meet him on the same bus and although no words were ever exchanged between them, neither was it ever reported to the orderly room.

I was amazed at the way JT eased his way about, and often I couldn't help but laugh at the things he did or said he did, though I never admired him for them. However, I never held it against him that he continually got away with murder. If he could get away with it, more power to him; but he remained, basically, a very unsavory person. I gave myself every chance to like him, even convincing myself that he would change overseas. Unfortunately, I was mistaken.

The next man in our squad was another person with whom we could have done very well without. He was Reuben J. Wolf, who was something of a lunatic, especially when drunk.

Wolf was from the Midwest, Minnesota or Wisconsin. He spoke with a German accent, which was certainly nothing against him. As is probable, he was raised among people from the old country and received little or no education except what he learned on the farm. Like Morris, there were times when you could talk to Wolf and times when you could not. And, like Morris, the times you couldn't was when he was drunk. I have never met a more violent person, one who went so completely beserk when under the influence of alcohol than Reuben J. Wolf. If ever there was a man so completely unhappy in the army, he was the one. The first day I met Wolf, he was drunk and no sooner had he taken one look at me when he began to curse me, calling me a prick, a sonofabitch, a louse and all the other sordid names he had in his limited vocabulary. I ignored him because he was drunk, and when I saw him again, sober this time, he spoke to me as though nothing had happened.

Sometime later, Wolf went AWOL for a few days and when the MPs brought him back, he was so drunk that they had to take him to the hospital. Another time, drunk as a loon, he borrowed a jeep from the motor pool and raced it all over camp until two MPs finally caught up with him. He was court-martialed, put to work at hard labor, and restricted to the camp. Then, one night, he got drunk again, walked into the orderly room, and grabbed Captain Porter (whose guts he hated) by the neck. By this time, he had been caught drunk so many times that he was brought to the hospital for observation. At the same time, his foot locker and every bit of his clothes were searched by a medical officer who thought he might have been acting under the influence of drugs.

They finally let him return to the company when they could find nothing wrong with him other than his weakness for alcohol. This time, Captain Porter restricted him to the company area and also placed a guard over him to see that he stayed away from the stuff. Even so, Wolf finally turned up drunker than ever though no one could figure out where he was getting his booze. They finally discovered that a woman he knew in town was smuggling it to him and that he was hiding his booty down in the boiler room. Even his old cronies, Morris and JT, admitted that Wolf was as crazy as a loon.

The last fellow in our squad was Bilyou, a kid from Highland, New York. Bilyou wasn't much of an asset either. There was something about him that I didn't like, a small kid trying to act big; and the more he talked the less I liked him. However, on the front lines, he turned out to be a lot better than I expected him to be. He was less of a boaster, did his work, and tried to be as helpful as possible in what he was supposed to do.

Our driver was Bob Walker, whom I've already mentioned. He had been with the Fifteenth Regiment at Benning and was assigned to the Fourth Squad in D Company when he came to Atterbury.

I would mention here a few of the others of the company with whom I came in contact and who pop in and out of this story. There was Sheppard who had been an ammo bearer in our squad until a few days after we arrived at Fairford, when one of the jeep drivers in the first section was hurt and Sheppard was assigned to take his place. He was a little fellow from Kansas with plenty of spark and was a good guy to have around. There was Turongian, a burly six-foot-plus from Utica, New York, who was built like a brick you-know-what. Bob and I tackled him one day, and it took us ten minutes to get him down. There was Tom Visocki, Section Leader of the First Section; Brummer, whom I've mentioned briefly; Sergeants Murfree and Hilliard, squad leaders of the First and Second Squads, respectively; and others, all of whom I'll give details as necessary in future chapters.

III

Of Razor Blades 'n' Things

It was a few days before we were thoroughly settled in Fairford, though never to our complete satisfaction. The park was a fairly small place with only four other companies occupying the area besides ourselves: B Company, C Company, Anti-Tank Company and Battalion Headquarters. The entire camp was fed through two mess halls. We used one together with C Company and Anti-Tank, while B Company shared theirs with Battalion headquarters. The officers ate in the old Palmer mansion which was used as Battalion headquarters.

There were four or five latrines situated at strategic spots in camp. These were average-sized barracks, the insides of which were lined with wooden seats placed over large tin pails. The pails were emptied every morning by two Englishmen who came by truck and gathered the deposit which, we assumed, was used as some sort of fertilizer. Four or five other barracks were used as washrooms. They were usually a good distance away from the living quarters, and on cold mornings the trip didn't seem worth the effort of normal washing. Instead, we found it easier to carry the water into our huts the night before and use our helmets to wash in. We had a shower room, too, which was located in the boiler room of the mansion. About the only necessity we lacked was a PX, which was a real necessity as it was difficult to buy anything in town. Even paper was hard to get, not to mention cigarettes, soap, toothpaste, and gum. However, ten days after we arrived, the PX was set up, and though we had to endure a long line to get our ration for the week, we were able to buy almost everything we wanted, including Coca Cola.

On our third night in England, Bob and I decided to go to town to see for ourselves what Fairford had to offer. We were all supposed to be restricted to the camp, from which only a few were allowed to wander each night. Guards were placed at the gate, but even those who had passes rarely used them. It was just as easy to climb over the low surrounding wall and dark enough not to be noticed. Once over the wall, a short-cut through the cemetery brought you into the center of town, where there were no questions asked.

Because of the blackout, and because it was such a small town, there was no activity at all in Fairford except in the pubs. If there is nothing else in an English town, there is always a pub, and there were several in Fairford. Bob and I walked down the narrow, winding streets into one place, where we ordered some beer. They were out of beer and suggested cider. We took the cider instead, but it was warm and not particularly satisfying, so we drank half of it and moved on to another pub.

In the second pub, we found JT. Though JT didn't have a cent to his name, he was one that could make the most of it. Equipped with a few double-edged razor blades, he made his way into the first pub he saw and, after acquainting himself with one or two of the local, unsuspecting, citizens, proceeded with as neat an act as was ever presented at a circus side-show. Gathering everyone in the pub around him with the craftiness of a barker, he pulled out a razor blade and offered to bet anyone a couple of Guinnesses that he would eat the razor blade. Those who were skeptics and those who merely wanted to see him do it just for laughs were more than eager to buy him a mugful. Then JT would slip the blade in his mouth, munch it for a long minute, and when he finally opened his mouth again, the razor blade had disappeared. Everyone was amazed and JT was offered all the Guinness he could drink.

There really was no trick at all to what JT had done, although, here again, we were skeptical. Masterfully, he had supposedly crunched and crushed the blade between his teeth until it was fine enough for him to swallow it, and anyone who doubted that he had placed the blade in his mouth to begin with was surprised to watch JT dig samples of it from between his teeth to prove that he was no fake. How his stomach was able to absorb it is still a mystery except that soon after his act, JT would swallow some lemon extract, presumably, to help decompose the metal in his stomach. He once offered to eat an electric bulb down to the metal for a couple of pounds, and even the metal for an extra pound, but no one ever proved willing to take him up on it.

Bob and I lingered in this place for a while, then tried another. Finally, after seeing what there was to see of the town at night, we went back to camp, retracing our path through the cemetery and over the wall.

During our first week in Fairford, we did almost nothing other than an hour's exercise per day and a two-hour daily hike through town and nearby countryside. Lt. Houghton, platoon leader of the First Platoon was our athletic director, and a very zestful one at that. Every day, for one full and continuous hour, we did every exercise conceivable from finger movements and neck twists to pushups, both benders, and rat races. Lieutenant Houghton, no slacker, and a pretty rugged fellow himself, did all the exercises along with us, and if at times he noticed us weakening, he exercised us all the harder. We did this in such a way that everyone enjoyed it, including me, which is saying a lot, since I never cared for excessive work, nor for that matter, Lt. Houghton.

Though my dislike for Lieutenant Houghton may have been a personal one, I did admire him for the energetic, eager beaver, whoop-de-doo person that he was. Houghton's main fault was his ego. He had taught the machine gun in ROTC for two years and knew every nut and screw of the gun by its catalogue name, knew every functioning movement of the mechanism, and could spit out definitions like a walking army manual.

This was all very fine, and one can't blame him for trying to teach the men every bit that he knew. But once the information was imparted, he expected everyone to know it as well as he did. If someone didn't give him a correct answer to a question, he would make a fool of the man in front of everyone, ridiculing him to the point where he couldn't answer any questions at all. Often, his remarks took on a personal nature, and he made several enemies in the process. He had a terrible way of making people feel uneasy in his presence. It pleased me very much that he was not placed in command of the Second Platoon, for we would have never gotten along. He knew too much to suit me, and though I could field strip the machine gun with ease, could detect the likely cause of any malfunction, and knew a good part of the functioning movements, his very presence shook me up so, it made me forget almost everything I ever knew.

In all fairness to Lt. Houghton, however, he was a good man to have in the company. His greatest accomplishment was not with the machine gun but with his daily exercise program. I believe that several people owed their lives to him because of these exercises, for our own physical fitness later proved to be a major factor in determining our own existence. And as I've heard since, Lt. Houghton turned out to be an excellent officer in combat.

Our own platoon leader, Lt. Knecht, was almost the opposite of Lt. Houghton. To begin with, when Lt. Knecht was first assigned to our company, he didn't know the breech-lock from the head-space of a machine gun. He was a relatively old army man of eight years service but had served most of it behind a desk or in some other branch of the service, possibly headquarters. When he took charge of the platoon in the latter part of September, he admitted that he didn't know a darn thing about the machine gun and was depending on us to teach it to him. Meanwhile, he devoted most of his spare time to studying the manual. During classes on the operation of the gun, he would let Sgt. Griffin or Sgt. Photenhaur conduct the class while he sat and listened, often more attentively than most of us.

Indeed, within a very short while, he had learned as much as most of us and more than a lot of us. In time, Lt. Knecht proved to be one of the more outstanding officers in the company, and in my opinion, probably prejudiced, more outstanding than Lt. Houghton, if only for his paternalistic attitude.

I always liked Lt. Knecht, as did most everyone in our platoon with the possible exception of JT, who didn't care for many of us anyway. When he first took charge, we all wondered what kind of a bloke they had given us this time. I might mention that our platoon had never had a platoon leader for any length of time. For some reason, they never lasted with us for more than a month, and usually they lasted for a lot less time than that. But Lt. Knecht knew how to win respect, and though he was outwardly friendly, he made it quite clear that he was no fool. He had a great deal of respect for most of the enlisted men and probably less for the officers, most of whom came directly from officers' school. (He was a first lieutenant and used his rank occasionally on the second lieutenants, which most of ours were). His informality in England helped him win many friends. Furthermore, whenever there was a break coming, Lt. Knecht was always in there fighting, making sure that his platoon was getting its share, even if he had to use his seniority to do it, and always willing to help his men along.

It was during our second week in Fairford that we learned that four-day furloughs would be given out. It was to be a volunteer proposition, four men to be allowed to go from each platoon at a time. Oddly enough, almost no one seemed to want to go on the first list; everyone was either broke or had just enough to last him for a few Guinesses in Fairford. Though we were broke too, Bob and I volunteered for the first list. Volunteering also were Yuskie, who was second gunner of the First Squad, and Hilliard, who was squad leader of the Second Squad.

The question was, where were we going to get the money? Sandviet was a likely candidate as he had won plenty one night in a crap game. Bob asked him, but we were a day late, as he had lost it all the night before in a crap game with Yuskie. I asked Yuskie and managed to squeeze a pound out of him, the equivalent of four dollars, which was hardly enough even to go on furlough at Fairford, next door. With Sandviet out of the question and Yuskie tapped as dry as he permitted himself to be, our chances for going on furlough looked slim indeed. Finally, we had to tell Griffin to have our names scratched from the list.

But Griffin wouldn't hear of it. He insisted we ask Lt. Knecht for loan of the money as he had won a sizeable amount on the *Aquitania*. Despite the fact that I didn't want to do it, Lt. Knecht came over to listen to our problem. It turned out that he had sent most of his money home, and since he was going on furlough too, he didn't have it to spare either. But he insisted he would get us some money, regardless. By this time, I was getting a little embarrassed.

We were in luck, however. The next day was Sunday, November 11, Armistice Day. We were to have a small parade in town, but just before the parade, it was announced that we would receive the remainder of our pay for October of which we received only ten dollars back in Miles Standish. This was an unexpected break for all of us, and though we could have used the extra cash, we thanked Lt. Knecht and told him we wouldn't need the money after all. That night we packed our bags, dropped them off in the supply room, and went to bed, looking forward to the next four days.

IV

Oxford on Five Dollars a Day

The next morning, we were up at the usual time, ate breakfast at the usual time, and at about eight, while everyone else was called out to do exercises, we walked into the orderly room and picked up our furlough papers and some prophyactic kits without which we were not permitted to leave. We brought a barrack bag along with us into which we had thrown our bare essentials. In our pockets, we had something over five pounds, the equivalent of twenty American dollars. It wasn't much to have a howling time on but we considered ourselves lucky to have that much, and if we limited our expenses to five dollars a day, we could make it.

We walked down to the train station with Zeke and Willy, who were also going on furlough. They were going to London but our finances permitted our going only to Oxford, although we were planning to spend a day in London. I couldn't help thinking that had London known of Zeke and Willy's arrival beforehand, they might have possibly traded them for a night of V-2 bombings and considered themselves getting the best of the bargain.

We boarded the train for Oxford at about 8:45 A.M. and within a few minutes, we were on our way. Bob and I shared a compartment with Roy Hilliard and Bob Yuskie and played cards for a good part of the eighty-minute ride. At a station near Oxford, an elderly woman boarded the train and took a seat in our compartment. We struck up a conversation with her, and she told us some well-known tales of the blitz and V-bombings. She was a very calm, soft-spoken woman, much like the type we had seen in the movies. She did admit, however, something that few British movies ever did, that they weren't winning the war alone. "I don't know what we would do without your help," she said. "You have no idea how glad we are to have you boys over here." Yuskie offered her a cigarette, which she seemed to appreciate very much, and Hilliard offered her a piece of gum. She seemed to appreciate that most of all. She took the stick, broke it in two, and placed one half in her mouth and the other in her purse. Hilliard offered her the whole package, but she graciously refused.

When we arrived at Oxford, we immediately headed for the American Red Cross to obtain lodging. We managed to get a room for the four of us in the annex for which we paid one shilling six pence a night each, the equivalent of thirty cents.

It was getting close to lunchtime now, and we were getting hungry, so we decided to stay at the Red Cross and eat there. The Red Cross provided nothing extravagant in the way of meals, but on the whole, they were pretty fair for the small price of a shilling three pence (a quarter). The meals usually consisted of soup, a slab of meat, some potatoes, bread, lettuce, pudding, and tea. The meat was usually tasty, but we could have done without the pudding, which I considered tasteless.

After lunch, Yuskie and Hilliard decided to go on a tour of Oxford University. Bob was to look up his brother, who was in England, and if possible, was to visit him the next day. I decided to go along with Bob. Exactly where he was, Bob didn't know and had to find out. His APO number was our only clue, and so we tried the Red Cross first for help. The Red Cross told us it might take longer for them to locate him than might be desirable and referred us to an MP station. The MPs suggested the Routing Office, which was situated at the railroad station. The R.T.O. people were very obliging, and Bob was able to learn that his brother's APO was situated at Tidworth, which was some distance away and off the main line. The trip back and forth, however, could easily be made in one day, and we decided to go the next day.

By the time we got through tracing Bob's brother, it was time for supper. We met Yuskie and Hilliard again at the Red Cross. They had visited a few pubs on their way to and from the university, and Yuskie was ready with the basic details. The pub hours were from two to five in the afternoon and seven to ten in the evenings. Beer and whiskey were priced the same as in Fairford, and liquor ranged from two shillings six for a shot of whiskey to three shillings three for scotch. How authentic the scotch was, Yuskie didn't know, but that's what the label read anyway.

We finished supper at about 5:30 and found ourselves with nothing to do until the pubs opened. Someone suggested a movie, and we all agreed it was the best way to pass a couple of hours. The movie we saw was an American one, *The Story of Dr. Wassell*. More than two-thirds of the films shown in England were American-made and which the British enjoyed so much. One reason was that British production had gone so far down because of the war; but even before the war, American films were predominant. The theaters were much like ours, large, but with little trimmings. The one outstanding difference was in the scale of prices. The closer one sat to the screen, the more expensive were the prices. With the movies, the British were not able to shake the way of the legitimate theater.

At 8:00, we stepped out of the theater only to find ourselves in what seemed like the middle of nowhere. A dark, moonless night had fallen, and because of the blackout, it was difficult to see more than a few feet ahead of us. We groped our way up the streets, and Yuskie, leading the way, found the pub. Most of the pubs in England are not as easy to find as bars are in the States (at least it seemed so to a "tourist" going there for the first time), although there seemed to be as many. Usually, the entrance was much like that of a house, with a hallway inside from which several doors led to the pub itself. Despite the sign in front, it was difficult for the nonfrequenter to find one, and in the blackout, you needed a person with a strong sense of smell to locate it. This Yuskie had, and so it wasn't difficult for us to find the first pub in minimal time.

We had a Guinness or two at this pub, but because it was crowded, we decided to find another. As we walked out we caught sight of some girls laughing at us from an open door of an upstairs room. Somehow, however, they weren't as tempting as the prospect of finding another pub, and so we went our way. We asked a young teenager where we could find a good pub, and he directed us, for which we gave him a few cigarettes. This one was situated in a hotel and was somewhat cleaner and less crowded. We had some port wine and some more Guinness and beer. By the time we walked out of the place, we were feeling pretty happy. We dropped into another pub, The Queen's Arms, as I recall, near the railroad station, drank some Guinness until closing time, and then decided to go to a dance, which was being held by the Red Cross. By this time, we were quite drunk, as it was the only way you could get me out to the dance floor. Finally, we decided to get some sleep. On going back to the Red Cross, I remembered noticing a theme that was being played all over England. Every dark corner was occupied with couples that were doing just what might be expected of couples hiding in dark corners on moonless, blackout nights.

The next morning, Bob and I were up fairly early and at about 8:45 we were at the station waiting for our train to pull in. There we struck up an acquaintance with another GI who was going in the same direction. At about nine, our train pulled in and we found ourselves an empty compartment. Then, just as the train was about to pull out, three girls, two WAAFs and a civilian, came running down the platform and jumped into the first compartment available, which happened to be ours. It was all very convenient, and the whole affair seemed prearranged. We struck up an acquaintance with the girls and found that two of them were also going to Tidworth. Surprisingly enough, neither of the girls knew each other which left Bob and me the only ones that did, a challenge which would quickly be overcome.

We were supposed to change at Reading and had a layover of eighty minutes, so we decided to go to a small cafe, where we had some tea and crumpets. The conversation that went on during that time, I really don't recall, but it was not particularly interesting or brilliant. The girls themselves were an odd assortment of womanhood. One, the civilian, was about nineteen and the best of the lot. The other soldier was taking care of her. Bob's WAAF was a good-looking number of about twenty-four. She was stationed at Oxford but was going on furlough, which disappointed Bob no end.

The one I had could have easily passed for a midget's daughter. I got stuck with her when I picked up her bag by mistake, thinking it was the civilian's. Actually, she was about four feet nine and quite plump, the way babies are plump at the early stage of development. Her hands were soft and tender, so small that I could actually close my fist around them. She was a platinum blonde, and her complexion was very light. It struck me that, for some unknown reason, this one had just stopped blooming at the age of eight. She was a lot of laughs, however, and with her peculiar cockney English, she did help pass the time of day.

Back at the station, Bob's girl boarded her train and a few moments later the five of us hopped ours. After a considerable ride we arrived at a point about five miles from Tidworth. There we dropped off my little WAAF as she had to catch another train. The remaining four of us then boarded a double decker bus which brought us right into Tidworth. We said good-bye to the civilian, wished the soldier luck, and went on our way.

Tidworth didn't look like much of a town. It hadn't been bombed, at least what we saw of it, but the place looked dreary, dirty, and decrepit. There didn't seem to be a decent-looking pub or theater in town. Situated along a hillside, it looked very much like a mining town, which it may have been, although we didn't stay long enough to find out. Immediately, we set out to find the army camp.

We inquired at a few places, found the camp, and were directed to the Locator's Office. The Locator was more than willing to help. Bob gave him his brother's name and serial number, which they looked up in the "live" files. When they couldn't locate it there, they looked for it on official papers but couldn't locate it either. Finally, after checking all the current files, they checked the "dead" file, that which contains the names of those who had been there once and had been reassigned elsewhere since. There they found it. Bob's brother had been shipped out on October 12, just a month before.

Bob, of course, was very disappointed. He had been looking forward to seeing his brother again, and the trip had already taken us six hours. We went back to the station and started back. We arrived at Oxford at about 9:00 P.M. had a bite to eat, and took in a movie. This one was *Bulldog Drummond Strikes Back,* an oldie but a good one. Then we went back to the Red Cross, where we saw an army show which had been thrown together by an Air Force unit, and we hit the sack.

We were supposed to get up early the next morning and together with Yuskie and Hilliard were to catch an early train to London. But the room was so cold and the bed felt so warm that we didn't get up until after ten. As the next train wasn't scheduled to leave until noon, Yuskie, Hilliard, Bob, and I spent some time in the building helping ourselves to some free donuts. At noon we were at the station. We boarded a crowded train, which left promptly, and finally entered Paddington Station at about two-thirty in the afternoon.

It was too late to visit any of the sights in London as we originally intended to, so again, we decided to find a pub before it closed. We had some fairly good whiskey and then hopped a cab, which took us to the more popular section of the city. We had a good dinner at a small restaurant, took an aimless walk, and again, decided to go to a movie to pass the time until the pubs reopened. The theater was the Odeon, one of the finest in London. It was a beautiful theater and between showings of the film, we were entertained by a twenty-minute organ recital. I felt that we were back in New York, sitting in the Roxy Theater or the Radio City Music Hall. The picture itself, *The Climax,* in color with Boris Karloff, was only a fair-to-middling thriller despite the picture having been chosen for the Command Performance that year, which was held there just a few weeks before for the King and Queen of England.

At about eight, the show was over and we hit the streets like a pack of hungry wolves. We had heard a lot about London's Piccadilly Circus and Rainbow Corner, and we intended to find out for ourselves. The place to start was a pub. The pubs were just as difficult to find in London as they were in Oxford, but Yuskie, old faithful, was quick to locate one. We were standing on a corner, when Yuskie slipped over to a nearby doorway. He lit a match, glanced at the sign above, and called us over. It was amazing, we thought, the way Yuskie could spot a pub. We all agreed that Yuskie just had a nose for those things.

After a few drinks, we stepped outside again just as two girls passed by. Yuskie and Bob slipped up next to them and started a conversation. Then the six of us walked over to another pub. The light in the pub put the girls at a gross disadvantage. Darkness was much more becoming to them. The better of the two was a blonde who claimed she was twenty-six years old. She may have been telling the truth, but we were inclined to believe that she was much older than she claimed to be; her leathery face appeared to have weathered many winters. The other, a hefty brunette also claimed the same approximate age. She too looked weather-beaten, but from her sturdy physique, I could tell that she could take a lot and probably had been.

We returned to the pub and remained there for some time, bloating ourselves with large mugs of warm beer and Guinness, and finally walked out of there feeling full and pretty high. The girls suggested that we go dancing, a suggestion that neither intrigued nor pleased me. I couldn't dance a step, but I decided to go along with the crowd. They led us to a dance hall a few blocks up the street that was crowded with GIs and their acquaintances. We found a table at one side of the ballroom, and

Hilliard and I sat down. Yuskie and Bob began roaming through the crowd looking for lonely waifs who might have been waiting to be picked up. Finally, Hilliard got up and asked the blonde to dance. I just sat there, squirming, my left arm resting on the girl's shoulder, my legs crossed, my body sprawled over the chair, and my mind thinking of what I was going to do if she took it upon herself to ask me to dance. I sat there waiting for her to say something. Finally, Hilliard came back with the blonde, and Yuskie and Bob dropped by long enough to tell me how silly I looked. It didn't make any difference to me, as I didn't even bother to sit up in my chair. The Guinness, having filled me up to my neck, was now beginning to fill my head.

The music started again and Hilliard danced with the blonde again. I just sat there, trying to figure out a way to ditch the girl. I could have done so by pretending to go to the men's room, but that seemed like a very old and very bad trick to pull. I was hoping that Yuskie would come back to relieve me of the baggage, but I knew that this wasn't going to happen the minute the girls had exposed themselves to the light. Yuskie came back to say only that he was leaving with Bob and that they would meet us at the station at midnight to catch the last train back to Oxford. It was inevitable. No sooner had Yuskie gone, when, suddenly, in exasperation I suppose, she turned to me and said, "Let's dance." Despite my protestations, she pulled me to the dance floor and beckoned me to just follow her.

What happened as we were standing in the middle of the dance floor must have been at least as funny as a Keystone comedy. My feet were like lead, and while we danced, she squirmed in silent agony every time I stepped on her feet. Instead of holding her, I leaned upon her. It must have been a funny sight as she dragged me across the floor and I tried to make believe that I was really dancing. Had they seen me, Bob and Yuskie would have doubled up laughing.

The music stopped. The ordeal was over. We went back to the table, and when Hilliard and his blonde came back, I suggested that we leave.

The girls lived on the East End, I believe, although I really don't remember. We took the underground and after several stops, we got off and started to walk. All the while I kept trying to make out with the brunette though my heart was hardly in it. Then, on a dark and lonely street, we stopped and I held her close.

"Don't do that," she purred.

"Why not?" I asked.

"Your mother wouldn't like it," she replied.

That did it! Finis!

"Let's go, Roy," I yelled to Hilliard. Hilliard wasn't making out any better than I was (he may have been taking a half-hearted approach also) and he agreed, leaving the girls to go home by themselves. We managed to catch the last underground back, hoping that it would take us to Paddington Station in time to catch the last train back to Oxford. But we arrived just one minute too late and had to wait until three-fifteen in the morning in order to hop a milk train that was going to Oxford.

We got back to the Red Cross at six A.M. Bob and Yuskie were sleeping, but we woke them up. "Say, what's the big idea of leaving us with those two old bags!" I said. (I was sober by now.) We all laughed and crawled under our cold blankets.

We woke up at eleven A.M., not because we wanted to, but because the maid insisted that she had to fix our rooms. After we washed and shaved, we had some chow and then looked for something to do. Bob and I didn't have much money left by now; barely five shillings between us and a ticket apiece back to Fairford. Then someone came up with a brilliant idea—a movie—and we spent our fourth afternoon in the theater. The movie this time was *The White Cliffs of Dover,* which was a good American movie, pro-British, though I don't know what the British themselves thought of it.

After the movie, we had supper, which Yuskie paid for, at an automatlike cafeteria. Yuskie was supposed to have a date that night, with three girls, no less, and he asked Bob and me to take care of two of them. But we decided to go back to Fairford. Hilliard had already decided to go back on an earlier train.

On our way back to Fairford, Bob and I recapitulated what we had done and not done on our four-day furlough. What we had done was to go to four movies, visited our share of pubs, and rode on a number of trains. That was stretching it! What we had not done was to see the sights of Oxford or London, which, if the days were longer, we might have taken in. (Besides the shortness of daylight, the blackout prevented us from seeing both cities at their best, the bombings notwithstanding.) Bob too, had not gotten to see his brother. Lastly, the prophylactics kit was still intact!

Anyway, it was good to get away from the environs of Fairford for a few days. Back at the "park," we told the boys some of the more amusing aspects of our furlough (Yuskie's nose for pubs, in particular), and by eleven-thirty, I hit the sack and was fast asleep.

V

"Mud Hill" Blues

The next day, we resumed our daily camp activities, which weren't too many but enough to keep us busy. They included a march around the town's Episcopal Church, known as the church with the most beautiful stained glass windows. But the windows had been taken out and stored somewhere, a precaution against air raids.

That day, Bob left for Liverpool, along with the other drivers, to pick up our jeeps which had just arrived there. On this trip, we lost one of our drivers, Wright, of the First Squad, who broke a leg in an accident. He was transferred to the Air Corps for ground duty. It was at this time that we lost Sheppard, our first ammo-bearer, who, via several minor shifts, became jeep driver for the Second Platoon. We received Bilyou, who became our last ammo-bearer.

A few days later, however, there followed a couple of drastic changes that were a surprise and a shock to most of the company. Griffin went on furlough a tech sergeant and came back a private. The way we heard the story, Griffin had gone to London with his dog tags in his pocket instead of around his neck. Colonel Descheneux, regimental commander, had suddenly issued orders to the MPs to check all enlisted men's dog tags and make sure that they were wearing them as dogs should. He was so emphatic about it that he promised to "bust" anyone who did not comply with these regulations.

Griffin's name was turned in, and he was reduced to a private. Captain Porter, who didn't like Griffin anyway because he persisted in doing things his way, didn't bother getting them back for him. Instead, Captain Porter replaced him with Sergeant Gerin, a master sergeant who had been carried by the company as extra rank. Griffin was assigned to the First Squad as jeep driver. Photenhauer was disappointed that he didn't get Griffin's old job. Almost everyone else in the platoon was dismayed, as Gerin was almost an unknown, and Griffin, regardless of what some thought of him, knew what he was doing.

When Griffin lost his rank, there were a few who were happy to hear of it and didn't mind telling him so. Among the first was First Sergeant Rowe. Griffin didn't like Rowe and vice versa. Both found common ground for their mutual dislike of Captain Porter. Rowe didn't get along with Captain Porter any more than Griffin. Apparently, though, Rowe had told the captain off once too often. A few days after Griffin lost his rank, Rowe lost his. Rowe was transferred to the mortar platoon of the Second Battalion where he became an ammo-bearer, and his place was taken by Staff Sergeant Olecki, a section sergeant of the First Platoon. If Griffin laughed to himself, it was understandable.

About a week after we returned from furlough, our squad equipment began to drift in. The First Squad received theirs first and, for a while, all the training we did with the machine gun was with the First Squad's which gave us less work to do in the way of cleaning equipment. Bob, meanwhile, was pleased to no end when he received a brand new jeep, as it enabled him to keep off company detail, a nuisance which presented itself every four days. Gradually, however, all of the squad equipment arrived except ours, which we finally received the day before Thanksgiving.

On Thanksgiving Day, our company had the misfortune to be assigned the entire list of details for that day. I wound up on KP which, on that day, turned out to be the better of the various details. I don't think I have eaten as much turkey in a week, most of it consumed between meals. JT managed to slip out of the mess hall with an entire turkey, but instead of taking it to town with him, as he had intended, he offered it to the boys, who tried their best but couldn't finish it.

Every bit of the meal was delicious, for which we had our own company cooks to thank. With all due respect to all the cooks in the army, ours were the best cooks, at least in the regiment. This was not only something that we all admitted, but also Colonel Kent, the battalion commander, and Colonel Descheneux agreed to. At Atterbury, it was not unusual for the Regimental staff to drop in for dinner or supper, and Mess Sergeant Charley Smith was invariably complimented for having the cleanest mess hall and the best cooked food. (This usually got us the first choice meats and the freshest vegetables.) Smitty, as we called him, was responsible for most of it. He not only knew how to cook food, but in his spare moments he would also help the KPs wash dishes or scrub floors so that they might get through earlier. With Smitty, it was help him out and he would help out in spades.

Smitty, of course, didn't do all the work. He had a good bunch of cooks who shared quite a bit of the burden of running the mess hall. Besides being good cooks, they were also "good Joes" and as comical a set of characters as I have ever met. Probably in no other part of the army set-up, other than possibly headquarters, was such a clique allowed to exist, and probably no other group got along better, not only among themselves, but also with the entire company.

Among the most likeable, and funniest, of the cooks was T/5 York. York was probably one of the wildest men ever to come out of the Southwest. Insofar as tossing quips was concerned, he was a perfect match for JT. Whenever JT would toss a volley of that particular Southern lingo, York came back with a volley from his own choice repertoire, which was often as good, and sometimes better, than JT's. Whenever the two got together, the KPs were in for a treat.

T/4 Pfaff was another character. He was a roly-poly, red-faced gent who spent much of his time outside the mess hall smoking a big fat cigar. He too could toss a particularly unique vocabulary, though he was not as boisterous as York or as loud as JT.

A little more reserved, at least in the mess hall, was "Red" Murphy, who didn't have the boisterousness of either York of Pfaff (or even that of Charley Smith) but was equally liked nevertheless. The remainder of the clique were two helpers who also did their share of the work. They were Jack Walker and Gene Saucerman, the latter an ASTP man from Fort Benning. They were rather reserved fellows when first they walked into the kitchen, but before long, their association with the other cooks began to show in their respective manners, too.

The day after Thanksgiving, we were surprised to learn that we were to start packing our equipment again. We were leaving England for France. It was indeed a surprise. We had not expected to leave England so soon. In fact, we had not expected to leave until March or April, when we expected the war to end. We were strictly "occupation duty" type, we thought. Who in hell wanted the 106th up at the front anyway? We would surely mess up the works!

Nevertheless, within two days, we were on our way. On the morning of the 28th, the drivers and assistant drivers (ours was JT) left for Liverpool with our jeeps and full battle equipment, which included several cases of ammunition and hand grenades. We left the following morning at about four with full field regalia and barracks/bags. After several hours, we boarded the train at Fairford station and, after a two-hour ride, arrived at Southampton at ten-thirty. At the docks, the rest of the regiment was waiting to board the ship, a converted Channel ship, and by 4:00 P.M. we were on our way to France.

The new ship we boarded was less than half the size of the *Aquitania,* but it carried more per square foot of area. Conditions were even more crowded here than they were on the *Aquitania.* Every hold (there were three) was a mess hall and sleeping quarters combined. Each hold had several tables and each table had twenty-four men assigned to it. At chow time (twice a day), everyone would assume his seat while two men left to pick up the meal. After chow, two others would clean the table, someone else would bring back the pots and pans, while another swept the floors. When it was time to go to bed, everyone would make a mad rush for the hammocks, throw the ends around the overhead pipes, and spend the night rocking themselves to sleep.

The meals aboard the ship were no better than they were on the *Aquitania,* but we were inclined to overlook this, since we didn't expect to spend much more than a day on board. When it developed that we were to spend five days, we really began to moan. The only thing we kept looking for at mealtime was the half of a loaf of freshly baked white bread which was truly delicious. Soon, however, our ration was cut to a quarter of a loaf, and we found nothing to look forward to.

The next day, at about noon, we arrived at Le Harve and dropped anchor in the bay. We were to disembark that night, we were told, if the water wasn't too rough. But the water was too rough that night and the next night too and the night after that, until we thought we would be stranded there for who knows how long. Finally, in the wee hours of December 3rd, we were told that we would definitely disembark. A couple of LCIs came abreast, and we were packed solid on the flat-bottomed boats. "Packed" is a word I use conservatively. From three to four hundred men, each carrying full field packs, were squeezed into each LCI, one section of which was devoted to barracks bags.

The LCIs (Landing Craft Infantry) steered through the harbor and finally coasted up to a rocky beach. Its front was lowered and being near the front, I was one of the first out. Lt. Bryce of C Company was ahead of me. He had his rifle over his shoulder and was carrying his bag with the other hand. Just as he was stepping out of the boat, a big wave came and threw Lt. Bryce completely off balance. Caught by surprise, he fell right on his face; his rifle, submerged in the salty brine of the Channel waters along with his baggage. He was completely soaked to the skin. I got a big laugh out of it, and so did everyone who saw him topple. More than comical, they were glad to see him soaked, for Lt. Bryce was one person whom no one seemed to like, least of all members of his own company.

When the entire company was finally gathered at the beach, we began to walk down what must have been a fashionable "l'ungomare" or seaside avenue. What it looked like now, however, is difficult to describe. Le Havre looked like it had undergone a half dozen San Francisco earthquakes. There wasn't a building a half mile from shore that could boast of an unshattered window pane. The walls of those buildings that were still standing were punctured with the countless thousands of little blotches so characteristic of fifty-caliber machine gun bullets. Along the beach were the remains of heavy gun positions, and there was hardly a camouflaged pill box that hadn't been blasted.

We walked about two miles, during which time we didn't see a solitary French man or woman. By this time, we had walked ourselves to the point of exhaustion and were happy to see several two-and-a-half-ton trucks come down the street to pick us up. We piled in, twenty-five to a truck, and were glad to get a little rest. We didn't go very far, however, and about twelve miles down the road, we got off only to find ourselves in the middle of nowhere. Obviously, this was the wrong place they had taken us, but the drivers insisted that they could do nothing about it, as they were merely obeying instructions. They left, leaving us standing there in the cold December wind, our officers wondering what they were supposed to do next. Finally, we were told to pitch tents along the side of the road. Just as I got my pack unrolled, we were told to pack up again, as we were going to be picked up soon by some other trucks. We huddled behind a barn for at least an hour, until finally, at 4:30 A.M., the trucks arrived. We piled in any old way, so glad were we to get out of the cold.

I fell asleep a few moments after the trucks began to move, and I didn't wake up until 8:00 A.M., just as we were passing through a little French town. Two hours later, we arrived at our destination, a muddy field on one side of the road along which the entire division was encamped. A nearby road sign read, "Rouen, sixty-five kilometers."

It was here that we met our jeep drivers again. They had arrived the night before. Their LSTs had brought them up the

Seine to Rouen, heretofore an unprecedented happening, and they had to drive from there. They also had been stranded in the Channel, but had found cause to enjoy it. The food, they said, was something outside of this khaki world. They were fed three times a day, and their meals consisted of roast chicken, steaks, blueberry "pahi," and ice cream, while coffee, good coffee, was available to them at any time of the day on a serve-yourself basis. I kept thinking about our own meals.

We pitched tents at one of the drier spots in the field. No sooner had we done this when it began to rain. "It's going to be misery if this keeps up," I told Grizzle who had pitched tents with me. "God damn France," he drawled. "They told me it'd be like this."

The rain did keep up. It rained in torrents for a while and then stopped, then rained again, then stopped, and while it rained and stopped, the mud grew thicker and thicker until that muddy field was christened and cursed "Mud Hill," a name which it rightfully deserved.

We remained approximately five days on Mud Hill, during which time we did almost nothing but curse France, its weather, and its soil. One day, we took a short hike to a nearby village, where we saw a small hill of apples that had been laid to ripen in the yard of an old farmhouse. That night, Charron and I made our way down to the house and piled a good share of the apples in a barracks bag. Some of the boys, meanwhile, had found farmhouses where they had little else to do but bargain for a meal or a bottle of cognac. JT found one place where he could get five bottles of cider for a few cigarettes, a loaf of bread for seven French francs, and a live chicken for a few francs more. The farmer's wife there also served him dinner, bathed him, and fitted him with slippers as he sat by the fireplace. "Damn hospitable, these French," said JT.

Despite the rain and the cold, we were just beginning to get used to Mud Hill, when suddenly, word came that we were moving up to the front. The idea of moving up to the line didn't frighten me, nor did it seem to have much effect on anyone else. It intrigued me, and I wondered what it would be like.

By eight on the evening of December 7th, we were all packed and ready to leave except for our tents, which we were allowed to keep open because of the rain. I had been on detail all day, helping the kitchen to pack, and now, a few of us, including me, were sitting around a small fire baking spuds. Suddenly Sgt. Olecki came up.

"Say, how about you boys doing me a favor?" he asked. "It's a half-hour job." (Everything was a favor for Olecki, and everything was a half-hour job.)

We all looked at each other, knowing we would end up doing it anyway, and scornfully asked, "What?"

It seems like regimental supply was sending a truck down here. We were to hop on the truck, go a couple of miles with it, load it up with K rations and come back. That was it. "Maybe you can slip off with a couple of K rations for yourselves," Olecki added, trying to make the job look more appealing. We agreed to do it (what else could we do?) and offered that if there were any more details coming up, we were already on one.

Charron, Turongian, Wells, and I slushed our way through the mud down to the road. The truck came and we hopped on. Inside were a few bags of potatoes. We ripped a hole in one and stuffed our pockets with spuds. A couple of miles down the road, we loaded about 135 cases of K rations and started back. When we got back, there was no one around who seemed to know what to do with the rations, or even if they belonged there. We asked the driver, but he didn't know either and took off to get something to eat at a nearby mess hall.

"What are we supposed to do now?" asked Turongian, directing his words at no one in particular.

"Hell if I know," replied Charron.

"I'll go find the driver," said Wells.

I might add here that with all the misfits and wild men the company had, Wells was probably one of the wildest, even when

sober. He was in Hilliard's squad and probably the most irre-
sponsible person I ever met. He once drove ninety miles an hour,
from Atterbury to Indianapolis so that a couple of guys could
catch a train back home. It was a generous gesture, but the
things that he did, and said he did, made even JT shake his head.

Wells came back a few minutes later.

"Okay, let's go," he said.

"Let's go?" I asked.

"Yeah. The driver said it's okay, we can go."

"Well, let's go," said Turongian.

Though we should have known better, we took Wells at his
word and went back. No sooner had we started baking our spuds,
when Olecki came running up to us again.

"Say, what in hell's the matter with you guys? Lt. Swick is
blowing his stack. He wants you to go back and unload that
truck." Olecki had gotten his dander up.

"But somebody said we could go," we protested.

"Hell, nobody told you to go back."

"Why don't you get somebody else. We broke our back lifting
those cases."

"Swick says he wants the same men."

"Ahhh—*/#*%. . . ."

So we went back.

"I thought you said we could go, Wells," said Turongian.

"That's what the driver said," snickered Wells.

"You never even asked the driver, you dumb */#*%."

Lt. Swick gave us a bawling out and told us that since we
were wise guys, we'd have to wait for the next truck and unload
that too. When the next one was due, he didn't know; maybe
two, three, or four in the morning. We unloaded the current
cases and began unpacking them, cursing Wells, Olecki, and
Lt. Swick.

The second truck never did come and at 4:00 A.M., I packed
the rest of my equipment and threw it on the jeep. I couldn't
wait to get started so that I could take off my shoes and change
my socks. My feet were soaked and had been that way for five

days. They were frostbitten too, had swelled somewhat, and were beginning to hurt.

By seven A.M., we were all set to go. The drivers were given maps which they were to follow should they lose the convoy. By nine, the convoy began to move out of Mud Hill. The 106th Division was on its way to take part in history!

VI

"Hey, Mom, I'm Hanging My Clothes on the Sigfried Line"

The trip through France was a fairly pleasant one for those of us who rode in jeeps. The gunners were getting a break this time, while the squad leaders were forced to ride in misery on crowded trucks. We were crowded too, and though Bob and I were in comparative comfort in front, poor Lum barely found room to seat himself in back where we had thrown most of our personal equipment.

Riding in a jeep through wide open country in December can be a pretty cold proposition, but we managed to keep warm by tying tent halves around the jeep, keeping our little squad stove burning at all times. The stove gave off quite a bit of heat which the tent halves kept from escaping, and we were pleasantly warm for most of the trip. As soon as the convoy got under way, I removed my shoes and socks and wrapped my feet in a warm blanket. The stove came in handy, too, in drying my socks. We had more than the comforts that one might expect on such a trip, and indeed, we found the jeep to be a better home than the pup tent on Mud Hill.

I don't remember the exact route we followed through France other than it was directed southward for part of the way. I looked at Bob's map only once, long enough to remember that we were to pass seven miles from Paris. Then, upon reaching a point in northern France, we were to swing eastward, through Marche, Rochefort, and LaRoche until we reached our destination which was to be St. Vith, Belgium. The French countryside looked pleasant, and the villages, quaint. At one point, we met a few villagers who waved wine bottles at us, but unfortunately, we were going too fast to stop or even to slow down to accept them.

As we had nothing to do but ride for two days, we amused each other by telling all sorts of odd jokes, of which Lum had quite a repertoire. He provided most of the hearty laughs and, at one time, kept us roaring with laughter as he tried to urinate in his helmet while the jeep bounced down the road.

The funniest incident of the trip, however, occurred that night. We had traveled about half the distance from Mud Hill to St. Vith and stopped for the night just outside a small town in northern France. Bob needed some rest, and Lum volunteered to stay awake until our supply of gasoline was replenished for the next day's trip. At about 2:00 A.M., the motor sergeant, "Pudgy" Anderson, handed Monroe a ten-gallon can with which to refill the tank. Monroe took the can, unscrewed the cap from the tank that was under the driver's seat, and watched the orange liquid flow into the tank. When the tank was filled to capacity, he replaced the cap, threw the can in the trailer and went to sleep.

Early the next morning, just after daybreak, the convoy started to move again. Bob turned on the ignition and stepped on the accelerator. But the motor wouldn't turn. He tried it again and again, but still the motor wouldn't turn. Finally, Bob called Sgt. Barnak, the motor pool mechanic, to find out what was wrong. Barnak looked at the plugs and wires and anything else that might be wrong and scratched his head. Finally, he decided to take a look in the tank.

No sooner had he put his nose near it, when he cried, "What in hell have you got in here?"

"The gas they gave me last night," replied Monroe.

"Gas, hell!" cried Barnak. "This is cider!"

A can of cider had apparently gotten mixed up with the cans of gasoline. Since cider has the same color as eighty-octane gasoline, the possibility that it contained anything but gas was the furthest from Monroe's mind as he poured it into the tank.

It took Barnak some time to pump the cider out of the tank and carburetor while the rest of the convoy passed us by. As a result, our jeep was four hours late in arriving at St. Vith that night. (It suddenly struck me that the incident would have never happened had Yuskie refilled the tank. After all, he had a "nose" for such thing.)

It began to snow as we passed through Belgium that afternoon, and by the time we arrived at St. Vith, it was snowing so hard that I had to work the windshield wiper by hand so as to remove the snow the moment it hit the glass. We were stalled just outside of St. Vith for over an hour because of congestion at the intersection ahead of us. At this time, Lt. Fisher of the mortar platoon, who was in the truck in back of us, crawled out and decided to take refuge with us in the jeep.

"I hope I'm not crowding you," he said as he squeezed poor Lum to one side.

Monroe snickered and said no.

Then Lt. Fisher went on to tell us of his troubles, of how cold it was in the truck and how uncomfortable it was, and after making himself more comfortable at Lum's expense, he went to sleep. Monroe was now sitting on a field pack with his helmet forcing the top of the jeep. I could see him trying to get some sleep but all he managed to get was a stiff neck.

When we moved again, we were directed to a wooded area just to the other side of St. Vith that had been assigned to our company. The kitchen had already been set up, and the cooks were readying a watery stew. Bob parked his jeep not too far from the kitchen but far enough for them to have trouble finding us for details. We grabbed our mess kits, got some stew, and slipped back to the jeep almost unnoticed. Bob and I slept in sleeping bags that night, but Monroe fixed himself a tent which was low enough to hold back the snow. Fisher went back to look for his platoon.

The next morning I was awakened, only to discover I was on KP, that I had to pitch a tent with the rest of the company so that the squad leader could find me, and that there was going to be a gun inspection. I resigned myself to all this but told Olecki he ought to get some permanent KPs. I gathered my equipment and dumped it in a spot near Grizzle's tent. Monroe said he'd pitch a tent for both of us, and I went down to the kitchen. I found Turongian, Brummer, and Malinowski also on KP. They weren't thrilled with the idea either, and we spent most of our time grumbling, much to the annoyance of Charley Smith and Lt. Houghton, who, among his other duties, was also our mess officer.

After lunch that day, I took a few hours off when JT volunteered to take my place so he wouldn't get stuck on some other detail. During that time, I managed to dry some heavy woolen socks and pass a brush through my gun. When I returned to the kitchen, I was bawled out because JT had made only a brief appearance and then disappeared himself. During that time, everyone else disappeared too, and Charley Smith was furious. When we were through that night, however, he handed each of us a can of pineapple juice and said he was sorry that we had gotten stuck that way but that on line there would probably be permanent KPs.

At about nine, I returned to my tent, and Monroe told me that I was on guard that night. Everyone was taking his turn for a half-hour, and my shift was from 3:30 to 4:00 A.M. This wasn't as bad as it sounded, as everyone had to get up by 4:00 A.M. anyway. We were moving up to the front. We split a K ration, drank the pineapple juice, and went to sleep.

Monroe had to wake up at two-thirty for guard duty, and I woke up with him. I took over at three-thirty, and when I returned, Monroe had already taken our tent down and was packing our equipment. A few yards away, Charron was packing and grumbling out loud in no uncertain terms. Lt. Houghton had thought that the gunners had it all too easy, getting up here in jeeps, and wanted them all to load the kitchen truck.

Cranky as I usually am at four in the morning, this latest bit of information didn't soothe me any and I burst forth with a long list of curses and damnations all hurled at Lt. Houghton.

When I realized that I was wasting my breath, I decided I just wasn't going. So did Charron. I gathered my equipment, walked down to our jeep, and threw the whole works into the trailer. Then I took my mess kit and walked back to the mess tent to get something to eat. I found that I wasn't the only one who hadn't reported to load the truck. There was no one there from the second platoon and the only people who were doing any loading at all were a few of the cooks and two men from Houghton's own First Platoon.

The meal consisted of pancakes that morning, all you could eat. I passed through the line twice, filling my mess kit to the brim both times. After I had finished a dozen pancakes or so, I helped Charron, who had passed through three times, to finish his. Thoroughly full, I returned to the jeep and sat there until it was time to get underway. I don't know how the truck got loaded that morning but nobody ever came by to ask for further help.

We pulled out of the woods at about 9:00 A.M. and followed the convoy as it made its way up the winding road leading to the front. This time, there were four of us in the jeep, as the squad leaders had been ordered to remain with the gunners. The mass movement of the line, which was fifteen miles in front of us, was a tediously slow process and our way was mostly uphill. On the other side of the road passed jeeps, trucks, and equipment of the Second (Indian Head) Division whom we were relieving. In a meadow to our right, we could see the 155's of the Second Division as they prepared to leave and make room for ours. One of them let loose with a parting volley, which caught us by surprise. It was the first sound of artillery that we had heard since we left Atterbury and the first sound of action that we had heard in Europe.

As we passed the Belgian-German border, we saw some Germans going to church, for it was Sunday, December eleventh. They looked at us rather curiously, though we certainly weren't the first Americans they had seen. Some managed a weak smirk and said, "*Guten morgen.*" We repeated the greeting and some-times added, "*Wie gehts?*" When they asked the question, we replied, "*Gut, bitte,*" but as our knowledge of German ended there, so did the conversation.

At about four o'clock that afternoon we entered a densely wooded area known as the "Schnee Eifel," and we knew that we were nearly there. The rifle companies and what remained of our own company had already vacated the trucks and were mak-ing their way to emplacements by foot. Our jeep sloshed its way over the muddy road until we arrived at a point where Bob was told to park, just off the road near what turned out to be a kitchen.

There we were met by a section leader of a heavy weapons platoon of the Second Division who told us to get our machine gun and follow him. Monroe and I removed the canvas from the trailer and took the gun and a few boxes of ammunition. Then, keeping low to the ground, as we were told, we followed the ser-geant.

First he took the First Squad to their emplacement, which was on one side of the road, and then he took us to ours, which was on the other. The sergeant told us to wait outside while he climbed down into the reinforced emplacement to get his men out. He emerged again, a moment later, followed by two gunners carrying their equipment. As soon as they had climbed out, we climbed in and placed the machine gun in the exact spot where the Second Platoon had just removed theirs. The sergeant pointed out our field of fire, our F.P.L., and some other vital bits of information and left us to have a talk with Photenhaur.

The quick change that took place in our emplacement took place in every emplacement along the twenty-seven-mile front now occupied by us. For the one brief moment that I saw the Second Division, however, I noticed a curious grimness about them that made me wonder. I couldn't make up my mind whether they were sorry or glad to be going. It had been two months since there had been any real activity along that sector. The sergeant told us that other than patrol work and the usual exchange of artillery, there hadn't been a single move by either side. The Germans were less than a thousand yards away and as well entrenched as we were. There hadn't been a man killed in weeks.

During these two months, the men of the Second Division had made living conditions for themselves as comfortable as possible. They dug large emplacements for the guns and then dug adjoining sleeping quarters. They re-enforced the emplacements with heavy logs to protect themselves from tree bursts and built triple-decker beds with thin logs, wire, and rope, which were as comfortable as anything we had in England. Heating was facilitated through improvised stoves made from water cans. In short, they had done their best to make their stay there as pleasant as possible.

It was, therefore, with some surprise that we watched these men of the Second Division emerge from their homelike emplacements in such grim fashion. Were they sorry to leave or had the peace and quiet given them a case of the jitters? Worse yet, did they suspect that this peace, this quiet, this aristocratic warfare was about to come to an end?

There were four cots in our dugout; Grizzle, Monroe, JT and I occupied these. Ten feet away was another underground dugout which housed Wolf and Bilyou of our squad and Morris and Ridgeley of the Third Squad. They had room for five men in their bunker, which included Photenhaur who had decided to bunk with them. The drivers were to sleep by their jeeps that first night and go back to the motor pool in the morning where they were used to division headquarters for whatever details might turn up.

It was fast becoming dark, and Grizzle went back to the jeep to pick up some extra boxes of ammunition. Meanwhile, we formed a guard schedule by which two men would stand guard at a time, two hours on and four hours off. When Grizzle returned, he gave us the password for the night plus some minor bits of information, and we went to bed, each waiting our turn to stand guard.

Guard duty that night was something new for us. Monroe and I kept our eyes and ears open, and if we were a little jittery every time the trees rustled, it was excusable. However, after a while, we became used to it and passed the time whispering softly among ourselves. Nothing happened that night, though we expected German patrols. Our artillery threw over a few shells, but the Germans didn't even throw one back.

The next morning, at breakfast, the drivers were readying to go back to division headquarters. I said so long to Bob and even thought about asking him for his home address. But it never occurred to me that this would be the last time I would be seeing him there, so I put the thought out of my mind.

Of the drivers, Griffin was the only one who remained with us. His duties were to pick up our meals at the company kitchen, which was two miles to the rear, and act as advisor to Lt. Knecht and Sgt. Guerin as he had so much more experience with the maneuvering tactics of a heavy weapons platoon than either of them. Our first meals, however, were to be fed to us by B company, to whom our platoon was attached. Our first one told us what to expect. Breakfast that morning consisted of one pancake and some oatmeal, the quality and taste of which left much to be desired.

At the B Company kitchen, I met Hilliard, who told me that he and Brummer had to stand guard all night. The same thing happened to Murfree. It seems that at dusk the night before, Visocki had walked back to the jeeps with about half his section to bring back some equipment and couldn't find his way back. Together, we walked over to the command post, where we learned that Lt. Knecht was getting ready to leave us to do some intelligence work for division. We were sorry to hear this. Lt. Fisher was to take his place. Fisher had been our platoon leader, briefly, at one time. He was a second lieutenant who was "bucking" for his silver bars for some time, and once the boys realized he was bucking, he wasn't looked upon with too much affection.

Fisher's stay with us, however, was a short one, probably the shortest ever experienced by any officer. He had no sooner finished giving us a pep talk, telling us what he expected when Lt. Knecht returned and told him to go back to his mortar platoon. Knecht wasn't going back to division after all. We were more than pleased to have Lt. Knecht. Fisher, however, was noticeably disappointed and secretly furious, not to mention embarrassed, at being shoved around, and rightly so.

I paid the Third Squad a visit that morning and found Charron and Durkin leaving to chop some wood. I picked up an ax and joined them. We spent most of our time talking about the Sigfried Line, Lt. Knecht, the B Company meals, and the situation in general. We were especially surprised at the inactivity around us. If we hadn't been told that the Germans were less than a thousand feet away from us, we would have never known it, as we had yet to hear them fire a shot. Furthermore, there was such an air of complacency in the platoon that few of us seemed to think that there was a war going on at all.

That night, I sat down and wrote a letter home. "Well, here I am," I wrote, "hanging my clothes on the Sigfried Line though you wouldn't know there was a war going on. We're living in barricaded huts, complete with beds and a stove, and it's the most comfortable we've been since we left England. At night we stand guard, and during the day we do nothing but chop wood. We don't bother them, and they don't bother us. This is a civilized war up here!"

The words were censored, of course (I have the letter at home). At any rate, those were my feelings along with several others.

The following day, Griffin brought us our first meal from our own kitchen. It was a pleasure to see good food again, and we ate a hearty breakfast. At the CO I met some of the boys from the First Section. I noticed that "Big" John Turongian was missing and inquired about him.

"He's back at the emplacement," replied Brummer, "afraid to get out of bed."

"Why?" I asked.

"He's scared," sneered Hammonds, an ammo bearer with the Second Squad.

"He's scared stiff," repeated Brummer, adding emphasis. "He was standing guard last night when he thought he saw someone creeping toward the emplacement. He pumped two bullets at him, and the figure stopped moving. When he went out there this morning to get a look at him, there was nobody there and no blood around either! He's been trembling all night. He won't stand guard alone and won't even get out of bed."

I was very surprised at what Brummer told me and was even sorrier to hear about it. I didn't expect this of Turongian. On going back to the emplacement, I met Charron. He had heard about it and felt likewise.

"Too bad," he said. "What makes it look worse is that he is such a big ape. If he was a little shrimp, they'd hardly take notice of it."

Back at the emplacement, JT had his bit to say about it.

"Why, the big guinea," he sneered (Turongian was half Italian and half Armenian), "scared as a rabbit! Thought he was a big shot at Atterbury. Now he's afraid of his own shadow."

"Go blow it out your asshole," I told him. It didn't seem to me that JT had the right to talk about anyone. "You don't look so fearless to me!"

"Are you sticking up for him?" he sneered. "Don't worry, you'll be dropping a load in your pants soon too."

"Don't you worry about me," I retorted. "Just don't let yours show when I'm around." I realized now that I would probably never get along with JT.

It was about ten-thirty that evening, and I was next to the stove writing a letter. Two men were on guard, though this time there was one man outside the emplacement and one inside by the machine gun. It was a little warmer than usual and the snow falling from the trees created sounds that were apt to give anyone the jitters. Suddenly, I heard JT calling me.

"Raffa! Raffa!" he whispered, rather urgently. "Come here."

He sounded excited, so I put down my pen and hurried into the adjoining dugout.

"What's the matter?" I asked. I tried to be as friendly as possible with him.

"Listen!" he said "Listen!" I listened but heard nothing.

"Listen to what?" I asked.

"Don't you hear it?" he replied in such a frightened whisper that it gave me the chills. "Don't you hear that ticking? Listen—tick, tick—hear it?"

I listened again. Sure enough, this time I heard a steady beat coming from somewhere close to the emplacement.

"What do you think it is?" asked JT. "I think it's a time bomb myself. These Germans are crazy, you know. One of them might have sneaked up here and planted a time bomb right next to our emplacement!"

I nearly laughed out loud.

"Bullshit!" I told him. "It's probably some water dripping somewhere." I gave him the best excuse I could think of.

"Man! That ain't no water dripping," insisted JT. "Listen, that sounds like a time bomb to me. I better wake up Grizzle."

"Dammit!" I snapped. "Let Grizzle sleep!"

I was beginning to get very irritated with JT. I didn't think he really believed it was a time bomb at all, but instead was trying to make me look stupid. It seemed inconceivable to me that someone who had gotten that close to the emplacement should bother to plant a time bomb when a hand grenade would have served the purpose as well.

"I'll prove to you that it's water," I said and moved to where the sound seemed to be coming from. I moved my hand slowly along the logs and suddenly felt water dripping on my hand. The ticking stopped. "There!" I said, pretty much relieved to find it myself. I showed it to JT and had him move his hand along the log. Convinced, he looked at me and gave me a wry grin. I returned to my writing.

I was pretty proud of myself. To this day I believe that JT was merely trying to make a fool of me. At any rate, if he wasn't, he was more of a fool than I thought he was. And if he was, I gave him no satisfaction, and it pleased me very much that I didn't.

That night, our artillery put on a big show, throwing tons and tons of shells into the German lines. One artillery observer at his outpost noticed the Gemans putting up a kitchen tent. He relayed the word back to his men with range and details and told them to wait for further orders. When he saw that the Germans had just about assembled their kitchen, he gave the order to fire. The first shell hit the kitchen squarely in the middle, and many Germans found it necessary to go without supper that night.

The next morning, just before chow, Grizzle pulled Monroe and me aside and told us that JT wanted to get out of the squad because he couldn't get along with either of us, me especially. He wanted to be transferred to the first squad, and in his place we would probably get Turongian, who had already been demoted to ammo gunner, Harwood having replaced him as first gunner. Grizzle asked us what we thought about it. I told him that as far as I was concerned, it was okay but as it involved me, I didn't want to say another word about it. JT, I offered, was just giving excuses to get into Murfree's squad, Murfree being about the only one in the company who thought he could really "soldier" when he wanted to. Monroe didn't care for the idea, and I realized that he was right. We had enough frightened people in the squad, he pointed out, referring especially to Wolf who had refused to stand guard alone. Turongian would be no help. At least JT could be expected to take over the gun if the situation demanded it. Grizzle himself, as much as he wanted to get rid of JT, was inclined to agree with Monroe.

At chow, I met Charron.

"Well," he said, "how are you and your pal JT getting along?"

"You know how it is," I answered. "You know JT. I don't know what he's beefing about. I haven't had any more arguments with him than anyone else has."

I was pulled aside by Lt. Knecht.

"What's going on between you and JT?" he asked.

By this time I was getting irritated at being asked the same question. JT had apparently told everyone he couldn't get along with me to bolster his own case and to get transferred to the First Squad. I blew my stack at Knecht. I told him that I wasn't the only one who couldn't get along with JT and that JT couldn't get along with anyone for any length of time, and I rudely walked away to eat my chow. Later, I saw him pull JT aside, but what he had said to him, I don't know.

Back at the dugout, I decided to have a showdown with JT, and we really had it out in words. It seemed that the more I spoke to JT, the less I thought of him. From then on, I said very little to him. "Low Life," as I came to call him, might just as well have not been there, as far as I was concerned.

There seemed to be quite a bit of activity on the German lines that night. We heard trucks and what sounded like troop movements, but in the morning, no one mentioned the noise and we forgot about it.

That morning, I met Turongian at the B Company command post, where a medical officer had arrived to examine the cases of frozen feet. Nearly half the company was there. The medical officer wasn't much help. His only prescription was "Keep 'em warm and bathe them in tepid water." Turongian's feet, however, were in worse condition than most of the others, and the medical officer took him back to the hospital to look at them. It was a break for Turongian, and it helped him considerably to get away from the lines for one day.

That afternoon, Charron, Durbin, and I chopped more wood, and when I returned, I got into another argument with JT, this time over the use of some V-mail stationary. Monroe also had a few words with JT, and even Grizzle was beginning to get annoyed at JT for his uncooperative attitude.

On guard that night, there was less activity than there had ever been along the line. Our artillery threw a few shells early in the evening, and the Germans let loose one or two V bombs in the direction of London (where they were launched from, we didn't know). At six in the morning, Photenhaur came running down to our dugout and told us we had been alerted.

"Why?" asked Monroe. "What's up?"

"Nothing," replied Photenhaur. "Just a dry run. The Germans have been known to launch an attack just before dawn and headquarters pulled an alert so that we know what to do in case it should happen."

Lum and I looked at each other and shook our heads.

"The 106th even dry runs on the front lines," I muttered. "When do we start policing up the area?" referring to a detail of picking up the empty shells after a firing drill.

Turongian came back about noon that day, although I didn't see him. Those who did said he looked pale and nervous. At about the same time, our executive officer, Lt. Roberts, showed up with our November pay. We played craps that day, and when I lost seven hundred of the seventeen hundred francs I had collected, I backed off, there being fifteen more days to shoot that month.

On guard again that night, Monroe and I commented how quiet it was. It was a little misty out and somewhat cooler than the night before.

"I bet you could hear a pin drop," I whispered to Lum.

"Yea," he replied. "Even the artillery's tired of firing at nothing."

At four A.M., we were relieved, and I went to bed. I was tired and my frozen toes were beginning to ache. I crawled into my sack, and before I knew it, I was fast asleep.

VII

The Battle of the Bulge

At about 7:15 that morning, December 16, 1944, I was awakened by Monroe, who evidently had been trying to get me up for quite some time. I opened my eyes and drowsily looked around. JT was warming himself by the fire; Grizzle's cot was empty.

"Better get out of that sack," said Monroe. "We've been alerted, only this time it's the real thing."

My eyes widened, and before Monroe could explain what had happened, Grizzle came lumbering down the ladder into the dugout.

"*Wall,*" he began in his usual drawl, looking as cool as ever, "the Germans are between battalion and regiment and between regiment and division. Except for a small area, we're pretty much surrounded." Then he looked at me and laughed. I sat up in my cot in amazement, and they began to tell me what happened since I had gone to sleep. I almost laughed myself; it was almost unbelievable.

At 5:50 A.M., the Germans launched a terrific artillery attack on our lines in preparation for an infantry attack that was to follow in twenty minutes. They had thrown everything at us from 88s to V bombs. Some shells landed so close that they thought B Company's kitchen had been hit. The entire barrage was ear-shattering, yet I had slept soundly through it, completely unaware of the attack.

I leaped out of my sack and painfully squeezed my frozen feet into my shoes.

"They want double guards outside and one by the gun," said Grizzle. "Raffa, you relieve JT in the emplacement."

It was cold in the emplacement, and I had to keep dancing to keep my feet warm. But I kept my eyes open, expecting anything to happen ahead of me.

I now realized that there was some fighting going on not far from the emplacement. I heard the crack of M1s carbines, and American light thirties, and the frightening rapidity of the German "burp" gun. This exchange of gunfire was taking place not more than 300 yards ahead of us, along what was our outpost. I could see no activity through the trees, however. Occasionally, a few medics would wind their way along the edge of the road up to the scene of the battle and come back with someone on a stretcher. Once I saw someone coming directly up the middle of the road with his hands over his head. *A Heinie giving up,* I thought, fingering the trigger in case it was a trick. But I was wrong. As he drew closer, he turned out to be one of the boys from B Company who had been shot in the hand.

Sometime later, I was relieved of my post in the emplacement, and I stepped outside to see what it looked like from up there. A sergeant of the Second Platoon from B Company was emerging from the woods with another GI and a wounded German who was begging for a "doktor." I asked the sergeant how it was going, and he said "Not bad at all. The boys up there are really doing all right for their first day in battle. This is the second German we've captured, and there are at least seven others lying dead out there. One of our boys got his head split open by mortar shrapnel, though, a few others are slightly wounded."

By afternoon, the firing had gotten no closer than it had been all morning, and activity on the outpost had lessened considerably. I hadn't seen the boys across the road all day, so I paid them a visit. They seemed to be no more concerned about the situation than we were. B. J. Vogel was busily heating some water to shave himself; Joe Sanders was in the dugout doing nothing in particular; Photenhaur was sitting by the phone; and Charron and Durbin were preparing to go out and chop some wood. We needed wood, too, so I picked up an ax and joined them.

We didn't go as far as usual this time, and we picked a spot that was well-defiladed so that our figures would not be seen while we worked. We talked and joked with our usual nonchalance and hardly even thought about the fighting. Just a big local attack, we thought, and that we were nearly surrounded did not make much of an impression on us.

Dinner was late that afternoon. At about three, Griffin brought back chow, and we went to the CP in pairs. There we saw Lt. Knecht looking at a German "carbiner" and a complete German army uniform. He had gone up to the outpost and shot himself a German. Lt. Knecht, up until this time, had been eyeing my pistol.

"Let me have the pistol," he once told me, "I'll give you my carbine."

But I liked my pistol too much to trade it for a carbine, and every time he mentioned it, I answered him with a curt "No, thanks." I asked him whether he was interested in my pistol now.

"No, thanks," he said, "but I'll trade my carbine for an M-1."

"What's the score?" asked someone.

"Well," he replied, rather hopefully, "they're still holding the escape route open and the 423d has swung around to protect our rear. It's not too bad."

Griffin was standing by his jeep, munching some food, and we asked him what was going on at battalion.

"Not much," he said. "But they blasted the hell out of regiment. Descheneux's sleeping quarters were hit, but he wasn't there when it happened. Service Company really got it, though."

We passed through the food line, received our cold pork chops, and returned to our emplacement.

Some time later, a few of us were milling around the emplacement when a B Company sergeant came running through the woods heading straight for the CP. A few moments later, he came hurrying back, this time with Captain Littlejohn, B Company commander.

Ten minutes later, both returned again. A long, drawn expression was on Captain Littlejohn's face. In his hand he held a steel helmet which had a silver bar painted on its front. A bullet hole had erased most of the bar. We stopped the sergeant and asked him what had happened.

"Lt. Bryce," he exclaimed. "Shot right between the eyes. He's lying out there waiting for the quartermasters."

A cold chill ran up my spine. Lt. Bryce killed in action! This was the first casualty among the officers of the battalion. What made me shudder, however, was not that he was dead, but the irony of his death. Lt. Bryce, a stern, cold man, was probably the most hated officer in the battalion. Several had promised to kill him the minute they were in combat. In England, he once found a bullet on his desk with his name inscribed on a tag attached to it.

Now he was dead, presumably a German bullet through his head. One member of the company who had been standing nearby coldly shrugged his shoulders.

"If the Germans hadn't gotten him," he muttered, "the boys would have." And with that, he walked away.

By five that evening, all activity had just about ceased. Only an occasional shot was heard crackling through the woods, but no one paid any particular attention to them. It was time for chow again, and Griffin had returned with some hot supper. Lt. Knecht had a little more news for us this time, news he had picked up via the British radio.

"They attacked us all along the line," he said, "from Italy to Holland. They've driven some of our units back a few miles, but Patton advanced four in an attack of his own. We're pretty well surrounded though."

This wasn't particularly heartening to hear, but everyone still took the news lightly. No one seemed to think that we were in too precarious a situation, and we had a feeling that some of our other units would forge their way into the ring that the

Germans had thrown around us and we would break out of what seemed like a flimsy trap anyway.

While at chow, we met some of the boys of the First Section. I asked Brummer what was going on around his way.

"Not much now," he said, "but there was plenty this morning. One little Dutchman is lying out there not more than one hundred yards from our emplacement. Looks like he was ready to heave a grenade when one of the riflemen got him. He's a sorry sight. Come down and see him when you get a chance."

I promised I would the next day. I had never seen a dead man before, and I wanted to see what he looked like.

"By the way," I asked, "how's Visocki coming along?"

"He's doing all right," answered Brummer. "He's either nuts or guts! He keeps running from one emplacement to the other, paying no attention to the bullets whizzing around. He's either too nervous or he's got no nerves at all."

I was surprised to hear this. We had always expected Visocki to go completely haywire in combat. As a garrison sergeant, he was little thought of by us. As a combat soldier, less was expected. Photenhaur, we thought, would make the perfect section sergeant in battle. I was really glad to hear this about Tom Visocki.

We had good chow that night, and I brought a mess kit back to our dugout to eat later, for I had gotten so that I wanted to eat five or six meals a day despite there usually being enough to eat at each meal.

Darkness came fast. Everything was quiet now. Hardly a shot broke the silence, and we had survived our first day of battle, though we were rather dubious about our positions. The riflemen had made a good showing. The enemy had hardly penetrated our positions. The B Company boys had taken three prisoners, and at least seven or eight Germans were claimed as dead on the field. B casualties were low: two killed and a few slightly wounded. As for us, the heavy weapons support, we had done nothing and had suffered nothing.

There was one thing that had been bothering me all day. What happened to the boys back at service company and our jeep drivers there. What happened to Sheppard, Tollett, Grube, and Bob Walker? Service company had been hit hardest of all. Were they hurt? Killed? Or had they escaped? I had a feeling that we wouldn't find out for some time.

That night, Monroe and I stood guard three times: from six to eight, from midnight to two, and from six to eight in the morning. As far as I was concerned, each of these shifts began at a "zero hour," though actually any hour could have very well been zero hour that night. Midnight was a busy time for patrols, and six in the morning was the German's favorite hour of attack. Monroe and I were ready and expected the worst. Monroe, especially, never stood guard without a hand grenade clenched in his fist. This time he also had a few hanging from the buttonholes of his coat, and I had a few myself. But the night was calm and quiet. We whispered less than usual and kept our ears a little more perky and our eyes a little more focused. Nothing happened. No stray Germans on our first shift, no patrols on our second shift, and when we expected them to attack again the next morning, there was no attack. Peace and quiet had returned to the front once more.

That morning at chow, Lt. Knecht sized up the situation. We were completely surrounded now. A small road was supposed to be open but of no practical use to us. Battalion had just about lost contact with regiment. Our water supplies were nearly exhausted, but there was still snow. As for food, well, there was still enough for a few days. Prospects weren't too bad, he assured us. The 423d was protecting our rear, and the Second Battalion, our right flank. The 424th, which had been in reserve, was supposed to launch an attack on the German lines in an effort to break through and make contact with us.

I saw Turongian at chow for the first time since he had returned from the hospital. He had come to chow for the first time in days and had been following Murfree so closely that he nearly stepped on his heels. He was pale and noticeably thinner, and his eyes were wide and staring. I greeted him and asked him about his feet.

"Not bad, not bad," he mumbled, almost in a whisper. Then he asked, "What's up?"

I told him what Lt. Knecht had told us. Turongian just shook his head and clenched his teeth. Then, urging the 424th to hurry up, he fell back into the mess line and got his chow, though I think he hardly touched it.

I started back to the dugout, a mess kit full of eggs in my hand. All the way back I kept thinking about Turongian. I felt sorry for him. Everyone was talking about him both to his face and behind his back. Were he anyone else, they would have paid minimal attention to him. But "Big John" was so big (six-foot-four-inches tall, about 230 pounds) yet he was acting like a frightened kid. I wondered whether he was really frightened or whether it was just a swelling of emotions that had been building inside him. He had told me once at Atterbury that he had seen one of his brothers, a machine gunner in the Pacific, come home from the war with an arm missing and his nerves half shot to pieces. Perhaps Turongian now saw himself as he saw his brother. He started to shake the moment after he fired those two shots into the darkness. He had been shaking ever since.

That morning, Durbin, Charron, and I set out to chop more wood. They told me about another fellow of whom we had expected much, our own Sgt. Photenhaur.

"I'm telling you, Raff," said Charron, cutting the "a" off my name as he usually did, "he's scared to death. He's afraid to stand guard. Oh, he'll go out at night for two hours, but he'll spend an hour and a half of it in the dugout. He explains that he's just warming himself for a minute or that he's forgotten something, or any other excuse. When any of us goes down to get warmed up, he complains that we should be upstairs on the lookout. He woke BJ up half an hour early this morning. You should have heard Vogel blow his stack."

"And what a pest he is too," added Durbin. "He wants you to do everything for him. It's 'get me this' or 'will you do this for me' or 'see if this or that—' What a pest! I wish he hadn't moved in with us."

I was very much surprised to hear this, and had not Charron and Durbin themselves told me, I would be inclined to disbelieve it. The more I thought about it, the more it seemed to me that there were very few of us on line who had remained unaffected by the attack. Some of us, who had yet to see a German with a gun in his hand, either never realized how close we were to danger, or didn't care.

That afternoon, we met Andy, one of our medics. He had a P38 in his hand, which was given him by a wounded German. We inspected the piece with much curiosity and then asked him about the dead German near Hilliard's emplacement. He agreed to take us down there and show him to us. "Don't touch nothing though," he said, "he may have been booby-trapped during the night." We borrowed some M1s and followed Andy.

We made our way down a familiar path to Hilliard's emplacement, and then Andy carefully led us through a net of wires and booby traps ahead of it. Had I gone alone, I probably would have set one of them off and killed myself. As it was, I nearly stumbled over a "trip" wire attached to the pin of a hand grenade tied to a tree trunk. When we reached the body, we decided to stay a good distance away, partially as it began to take on a stench.

It was as Brummer had described him earlier, a gory sight. He was lying on his back with his rifle beneath him. Apparently, it had been in his left hand and he was probably creeping his way up toward his objective. He must have been ready to throw a hand grenade with his right hand, though he hadn't armed it yet. Some alert rifleman had spotted him just as he was rising and sent a bullet through his head which emerged from his stomach. He apparently dropped both grenade and rifle, and in his agony, rolled over on his back. He died almost instantly, with his eyes wide open, his hands and fingers curiously twisted. His face looked waxy and pale, almost green now. When we had seen enough of him, we left, quite shaken at the sight.

That evening, Griffin brought no chow back, and each man was given a can of corned beef from emergency rations that had been stored at the CP. Included in these rations was a box of graham crackers per section and a can of corned beef per squad. We were completely out of water now and had to drink melted snow.

That night was a noisy one. Enemy artillery was at work again, hammering our rear echelons with all kinds of shells and bombs. One robot bomb came over so low that I actually ducked in sheer fright, although, actually, it was very far over our heads. For a moment, I expected it to give out and fall right then and there, on top of our emplacement. But it sputtered on, and I didn't hear it explode until some minutes later.

The next morning, Grizzle came back to us with the news that Colonel Kent, Regimental Commander, had been seriously hurt by shrapnel which had hit him in the back of the head. He was lying on his death bed. Also, we were told to gather our belongings. We were moving out. As for chow, there wasn't going to be any that morning. Griffin had gone back but had returned with nothing. The kitchen had given orders to pack and get ready to move out. B Company had cooked a little chow, and I had a few pancakes with them. Later, some processed cheese was passed around as well as a few crackers, and we managed to make a small meal out of it.

That morning brought a change in our squad. Lt. Knecht decided that JT might as well move to the First Squad, where he wanted to be, and we received Turongian. This was received with little enthusiasm by most of the squad, but I welcomed the change. Turongian was my friend, and I believed that he would eventually get over his shakes. Thus, Turongian became our first ammo bearer.

And so we readied ourselves to move out. What puzzled us, though, was where were we going? We were completely surrounded, and there was hardly any room to maneuver in.

VIII
No Escape

It was nearly noon when we finally started back. This wasn't a retreat, we were told, we were going into the attack! Our positions were no longer along the front, the lines were in our rear. Their lines were about seven miles deep, and the closest American unit, our 424th Regiment, was eleven or twelve miles to our rear. Within the area now occupied by the Germans was the little town of Schoenberg. We were to attack this town, units of the 423rd from one side and units of the 422nd from the other. At the same time, it was expected that the 424th was going into the attack from their positions. By virtue of this coordinated attack, it was believed that the Germans would be squeezed out of town thus enabling us to rejoin our own forces. Providing that everything went well, we were told—it was a cinch.

The march back was miserable. Much of it was uphill, and our equipment was a severe hindrance to us. Most of us were carrying full field packs over our jackets and overcoats. The full field pack was somebody's brilliant idea in battalion. "Take all you can with you," they told us, and everyone packed sleeping bag, underwear, blankets, and even an extra pair of shoes. I took along only my sleeping bag, some underwear, and a pair of socks in addition to my overcoat, jacket, and of course, my gas mask. All this was heavy enough, but it was only personal equipment. There was, of course, the squad equipment to carry, which was more important and certainly heavier.

A heavy weapons company may have it easy as it goes up to lines, but when it is forced to withdraw, it finds itself doing so with much greater difficulties than even the rifle company experiences. A gunner in a machine gun platoon carries either a forty-three pound, fifty-caliber (water-jacketed) machine gun, or a fifty-one pound tripod. A gunner in the mortar platoon carries either a tube, tripod, or base plate, all of which weighs over forty pounds. An ammo bearer in either platoon carries two or three twenty-pound boxes of ammunition or about sixty pounds of mortar shells. Even squad and section leaders have to carry their share of equipment. Being first gunner, I carried the tripod. Add the fifty-one pounds of the tripod to the weight of the pack, the coat, the jacket, the gas mask, the belt, and the pistol, not to mention the weight of the oppressive steel helmet pressing heavily on my head, and the awkwardness of the heavy artics over my shoes, you can imagine how I felt as we slowly progressed upward. A mule!

The weather didn't help matters much that day either. It was somewhat warmer than it had ever been before, and a low, heavy mist had settled over the Eifel. It was excellent weather to move about in secrecy (if you knew where you were going), but it was certainly no weather to go hiking in (especially if you didn't know where you were going). We had not trudged for half a mile, when we began to feel the effects of the humidity and began to sweat profusely. Packs and overcoats were cast into the snow in an attempt to obtain relief and ease the burden. I held on to my pack desperately for another half-mile, until I finally got rid of it too, salvaging only two cans of C rations that had been distributed early that morning.

Slowly, we trudged up along the same road we had used just a few days before when, new and eager, we rode up to our emplacements to take over this "quiet sector." Finally, we arrived to what was left of the battalion C.P., near a point where our kitchen had been located. Here we met the cooks who had abandoned all but their rifles, and the mortar platoon which all the while had been stationed to our rear. From here, a convoy of a few trucks and jeeps which had not been ordered to division and loaded with equipment we could not carry (additional ammunition, food, and a ton of officer's baggage) set off along a small road in the hope of making contact with the 424th Regiment. Along with the convoy went Powell, our platoon messenger. After a few moments rest, we resumed our march. "Just a few more miles to go," we were told, "and we'll get to an assembly area where we'll get some sleep and then jump off in the morning."

We hadn't moved many yards when the sweat began pouring down my back like so much warm water. I decided to get rid of my overcoat. Grizzle was going to do the same, but he decided to relieve me of the tripod and threw his overcoat on top of it. I decided to give it one more try and slid it inside the straps of my gas mask. What Grizzle gave me in return for the tripod, however, was no bargain. It turned out that instead of Grizzle relieving me, I was relieving Grizzle. I had to carry his M-1 rifle, a box of ammunition, and another full belt of ammo that had fallen out of a box. This belt I had to toss around my neck which was very uncomfortable as it gradually forced my head down to the point where my chin was almost resting on my chest, which literally gave me a pain in the back of the neck. The twenty-pound box also added to these miseries as it slowly strained my arm so much that I soon lost all power in it.

The real key to this equipment was that I was not properly balanced with it as I had been with the tripod. The tripod legs at least rested on both shoulders, and though it weighed more than all of Grizzle's equipment combined, it was a balanced weight and less of a burden. However, I managed to drag myself along and I lagged behind no more than the others. At one time, Wolf, tired of carrying his ammunition, dropped it along the road. When Lt. Knecht heard about it, he became furious. Not only did we need every round of ammunition that we had, but Wolf had decided that his pack was more important than the ammunition. This made Lt. Knecht so mad that he kicked and cursed him, made him drop his pack, and threw two other boxes at him to carry. He threatened to shoot him on the spot if he dared to drop these.

The journey back became increasingly difficult with every step. The long column of men began to move slower and slower. Luckily, we had several breaks along the way while Major Moon, now in command, Lt. Tome, Battalion G2, and the rest of the staff including Captain Porter stopped to gather their bearings. Much of the march took us through high bushes and twisted trees, and it was pretty rough going. At one point we came to a tremendous hill at least 200 feet high and with an inclination of some thirty degrees. How all of us made it up that hill, I will never know. (Lt. Houghton may have had something to do with it.) There were no footholds, and we had to pull ourselves up by holding onto small bushes, which often gave way under the weight of our bodies. Once you slipped, you found yourself at the bottom of the hill again. I crept and crawled every bit of the way. At first I tried to keep the ammunition from getting dirty, but I gave that up halfway up the hill. By the time I reached the top, I was so weary that I staggered all the way up to catch up with the rest of the squad.

The weary procession wound its way through some more high brushes and finally burst into a wide plain. It was dusk now, and the skies were already beginning to darken. We had to hurry across in this field, we were told, so that the Germans wouldn't spot us, and so we started across the field at a fast pace. Looking back at it, it was quite a chance we took. How the Germans never spotted us, I still don't understand, for over in the not-too-far woods at our left, we could hear the burp guns firing away in the other direction. Yet here we were in a column of twos stepping across the wide open terrain as though nothing was going on.

We cleared the plains and made our way across a patch of woods. About a quarter of a mile further, we came to a small clearing almost completely surrounded by woods. Here we finally stopped. C Company and A Company were waiting for us. The Second Battalion had also arrived. This was to be our forward assembly area. A stop here until the morning, and then attack. We were directed into the woods at the right, designated unit areas, and told to start digging prone shelters in case the Germans had spotted us and decided to drop 88s into the woods. (Had they done this, prone shelters would have been useless anyway, since tree bursts would have sent shrapnel firing down on top of us.)

It had become completely dark now; I could hardly see my hand in front of my face. I had no shovel—that had gone the way of the pack. I decided to use my steel helmet and began scraping the ground the way I had seen in a movie back in basic training. After a while of scraping, I realized that I was getting nowhere and concluded that the movie must have been a monstrous fake. Exhausted, I dropped the helmet and propped myself against a tree.

I was quite hungry by now, so I opened the "dry" can of my C rations, ate the crackers and candy, and decided to save my "wet" can (beans) until I really needed them. Finished eating, I was about to close my eyes for a little sleep when the order was given to prepare to move out again. In another five minutes, we were on our way to a more "strategic" area, this one some two miles away.

We followed the road back, again across that field, for about a mile and then turned in a different direction until we came to another open area. Here we stopped for a long while. Apparently G2 had gotten lost. In the distance were two different patches of woods, and he couldn't make up his mind which one he wanted to go to. This gave us a chance to catch up on a little rest, and we lay down, cuddled up in a row, Grizzle, Turongian, and I, as close as we could get. I appreciated my overcoat now, for it was becoming bitterly cold again, and those who had thrown theirs away were longing for them.

At about eleven o'clock we started to move again. G2 had finally decided that we go to the left patch. Mum was the word, however; absolute silence was imperative, for the Germans were only eight hundred yards away.

We reached the area designated, and much to our surprise we found three large shacks that were once an artillery G.P. and supply rooms. There we were to stay and get some sleep until 7:30 the next morning, when we were to make a "surprise" attack on the Germans. Our platoon was given one shack and the mortar platoon another. B Company was to sleep outside. Some were assigned to guard detail, and others went to sleep on the ground or on the roofs. Meanwhile, A and C Companies occupied other positions on a small ridge to our left. Again we were warned: *Silence!*

But there was no silence. No sooner had we entered the shacks, when everyone began to talk at once; about the break we had gotten to get out of the weather, about the march, about the impending attack. The commotion got to the point that Lt. Fisher found it necessary to come in and tell us to keep quiet. Lt. Knecht immediately reminded him that he was the officer in charge and Lt. Fisher left, enraged and embarrassed. Lt. Knecht then put a stop to the commotion, and we settled down to get some rest. It was past midnight now. I found a table to sleep on (it was well cushioned with great quantities of gun patches), which I shared with Joe Sanders. He had a can of K rations and I had a can of condensed milk, which together we made a meal of it. I fell asleep soon after and didn't even dream about that coming morning.

Morning came. At about seven-fifteen we were all awakened and ordered to take up primary positions outside. Meanwhile, we checked our equipment. Our platoon had four new machine guns; ours, in fact, had not been fired before, not in Atterbury or in Europe. I fixed the headscape but wasn't sure whether the gun would fire at all even though the trigger clicked when tested without ammunition. This was a hell of a time to find out, I thought.

Each gun had from five to eight boxes of ammunition, less than two thousand rounds per gun. The mortar squads were even worse off. They had twenty-four rounds for five mortars, all of them "H.E. Lights," a shell of lesser impact. The sixth mortar had no base plate. It seemed that one of their less brilliant men, a forty-year-old ammo bearer named Geer, had been assigned to carry it. Back in the woods where we had gathered, however, the forgetful PFC Geer had set it down, and when we left, forgot to pick it up again. When asked why, he exclaimed that he thought another sad sack, Crislip by name, had picked it up. The loss of the baseplate, however, was of little consequence with no ammunition. Actually, the incident provoked more laughter than alarm, for Geer and Crislip were two other characters one found difficult to avoid laughing at.

I picked up my tripod and set it outside. Monroe followed with the gun. Immediately, I realized that this attack was going to be no "surprise." The Germans were already shooting, and there seemed to be no semblance of organization among our ranks. The entire affair began to take on the appearance of a mock battle. Some of the men were lying on the ground, terrified. Others were sitting and talking among themselves. Still others were walking around as though nothing was happening.

I saw others, too, who were scurrying around, running into one particular shack and running out with food in their hands. I told Monroe to watch the gun while I went into the shack to get some food. I emerged with a gallon can of corned beef; most of the other food was vanquished by the bunch of hungry soldiers who had not eaten in a couple of days. Monroe, sensing that we might need it later, volunteered to carry it in a discarded ammo bag.

Finally, someone decided to get things organized. The riflemen were ordered to take positions behind the trees in any foxholes they could find. True to the printed field manual, which were the only tactics our officers knew, we in D Company, were given positions along the flank to provide protection. The riflemen opened fire, and two of our light thirties opened up, one of them Griffin's who had carried the light machine gun unaided all the way. From this point, the riflemen were to rush across a wide open field and capture the enemy positions along a road about 800 yards away. The Germans were firing back, however, and this never came about. To make the attack would have been suicide, since there was no defiladed area, or even partially defiladed area, in which the riflemen would hide behind. As a result, the heavy weapons squad, with our machine guns, were called up to give them fire power. Following Grizzle, and Grizzle in turn following Photenhaur, we made our way to the edge of the woods facing the Germans.

"Set the gun up there," yelled Grizzle, pointing to a foxhole about twenty-five feet in front of him. (Grizzle was making certain that he kept some distance away from the gun, for once it was set up and opened fire, it was a target for every kind of enemy retaliation.) I made my way to the position. There, I faltered.

The foxhole was no place for a machine gun. First of all, the hole was full of mortar ammo crates. Second, there were mortar tubes piled up in front of the foxhole, which made it impossible to set the tripod there correctly. I stalled for a moment; I wasn't quite sure of what to do. I was almost afraid to move the crates for fear that they might be booby-trapped. "Set up the gun," Grizzle kept yelling.

Finally, in desperation, I began setting the tripod as best I could. I had to toss it over the tubes and there was no way of supporting it at all. Monroe came up with the gun and mounted it on the tripod. Now I saw that it was impossible even to fire the gun in the position it was in. It was out too far, in full view of the enemy, and too high and very unstable besides. I had wasted a lot of time, but I had to get the gun in good firing position. Meanwhile, the Third Squad, with Charron and Durbin behind the gun, were already set up next to us, and Photenhaur, who was between us, was already giving them orders and directing their fire.

"This is a hell of a place to set up a gun," I yelled back at Grizzle. "I'm going to move it over here," and I pointed to a small space between the foxhole and the tree. Desperately, I tried moving the gun to the new position. But it was difficult. I didn't want to expose myself in full view of the enemy, who I felt must have spotted me by now. What hampered my movements, too, was the belt that I had left in the gun. Twice my shoulder accidentally hit the trigger and bursts of two and three rounds went off.

Finally, after what seemed to me like ages, I had the gun where I wanted it and ready to fire. Meanwhile, Monroe had jumped into the foxhole and worked the elevating mechanism while I worked the traversing mechanism. Photenhaur, who had become impatient, now yelled some firing orders: "Range 800! Aim right into the corner of that building and start firing!" I set the range, aimed, and squeezed the trigger, hoping for the best.

The gun fired perfectly, as I should have realized at the couple of bursts before. It was now getting its "baptism of fire" right up in combat. The aim was true, for no sooner had I fired when Germans began scattering right and left.

"Your bursts are too long!" yelled Photenhaur. "Watch your ammo! Give it a couple of more bursts!"

I did. But it seemed that my bursts were still too long. Photenhaur, it seemed, had gotten as disgusted with me as I had gotten with him.

"God damn it," he yelled, "Grizzle, take over the gun."

Almost reluctantly, Grizzle crept up to the gun. I left in disgust and crawled back to pick up Grizzle's rifle and field glasses. Then I crawled to another tree nearby and watched the firing.

"A hundred miles right," yelled Photenhaur. "There's a latrine out there that's hiding a lot of Krauts. Fire as soon as you're ready."

Grizzle set the gun and fired. He was fast and worked perfectly. His first burst entered directly into the latrine, and almost instantly, Germans scattered in all directions.

By this time, however, the Germans had spotted us and began aiming some mortar fire on us. The first one landed a good 200 yards from us, but each succeeding one came closer and closer. Then suddenly, the enemy ceased firing at us, and an order came for us to cease firing too. I wondered why. A glance to the right gave me the answer. Three tanks were coming up the road.

"They're American," someone yelled.

"No, they're British," cried another.

The tanks stopped and some men jumped out. They were met by six or seven people who were jumping up and down and animatedly pointing our way. I looked through Grizzle's glasses but couldn't make out either uniform or helmet, nor could I distinguish the nationality of the tanks. I tossed Grizzle the glasses.

"I don't know what the hell they are," he drawled after taking a look. "They look awful funny to me."

The tanks, of course, turned out to be German. It had been quite obvious from the beginning, though everyone hoped against hope that they weren't. Why we were not allowed to fire at them I didn't know. They made perfect targets, marvelous sihouettes against the morning sky, which is one reason why we really couldn't identify them to begin with. They were a gunner's dream. Never could anyone expect such an invitation. Machine gun fire would have surely wiped out a number of gesticulators and a few mortar shells could have been put to better use.

Then I realized why.

"Let's get out of these woods," yelled G2. "Once they train those 88s on us, we'll all be killed by tree bursts!"

A certain madness then pervaded. All was confusion. The riflemen, who hadn't even bothered to fire a shot all the while that we had been pumping away, began scattering in all directions to get out of the woods. The terrain to our left slowed down a big draw which was devoid of trees and by which ran a small stream. The majority started running in that direction, and soon, others followed. There was some defilade there, and we would be comparatively safe, at least from small arms fire.

Grizzle grabbed the gun, Monroe the tripod, and I picked up Grizzle's rifle and some ammunition and followed the crowd. We had barely vacated the woods, when the Germans began pumping 88 shells into it. They did the same in another patch of woods some distance away from which units of the 423d Regiment had not yet abandoned. Screams of agony could be heard coming from those woods with every burst of fire. The tree bursts were scattering shrapnel in all directions, killing some and wounding many of that group.

Getting us into the draw was what the Germans wanted. We were trapped there. Major Moon's plan must have been to retreat down that draw and then make our way over a hill to the other side where the Second Battalion was. He himself was the first to try it and make it. Captain Porter, Captain Littlejohn, Lt. Toner and Lt. Hotaling as well as a few of the other officers and enlisted men made it, but it wasn't long before the Germans got wise and trained their fire in that direction, which made it impossible for anyone else to clear that hill. We were now in a terrible position. There wasn't much room to maneuver it. We had to keep our heads low to keep them from being shot off. We lay there for quite a while, until someone up front decided to try and organize the unorganized group of us that were left. What happened then, in that draw, was both comical and tragic.

"Bazooka men up front," was the cry. "Bazooka men up front."

But the bazooka men had already thrown their bazookas away for rifles.

"Medics up front! Medics up front!" came the call. But the medics had suddenly lost all sense of hearing, and one couldn't blame the medics. One medic had already been shot trying to treat a wounded rifleman; the cross on his helmet had made a perfect target.

Lt. Fisher came crawling up to Lt. Mason who was hugging the ground like a pillow.

"Gather your men and set up your mortar!" he yelled.

Lt. Mason merely gave him a dirty look and hugged the ground even closer.

Then someone yelled, "Let's go back that way!" Half the men began starting back, creeping and crawling all the way and keeping as close to the ground as they could. One fellow was wading down the stream keeping his body well down to prevent being seen. Suddenly he came to a long, three-foot diameter culvert through which the stream ran. Afraid to make his way over the culvert, he decided to crawl through it on his stomach. It was both a comical and tragic sight. The poor kid was having a tough time of it. Unfortunately, I lost track of him after he entered, and I never saw him emerge.

Most of our platoon was following those that were going in that same direction, including Lt. Knecht, who had long before expressed his desire to retreat in that direction. Where we were going, however, nobody had any idea. Then came a cry that sounded like an authoritative person back in the draw.

"Hey, come back! You can't leave half the battalion down here like this!"

Again, some of us started back. By now we were just a mob of people, running around and getting nowhere. It reminded me of the game we played on the *Aquitania* while passing the time on decks. We were again in a small circle, bouncing from one side to the other, getting no place.

I, and several others, were getting tired of moving around like this, so a few of us decided to sit down in a clump of weeds and wait to see what happened. Charron and Durbin were already sitting there and Sgt. Visocki was standing nearby. We were exhausted and tired, disgusted with the entire situation. Suddenly Visocki's loud voice penetrated my ears.

"Oh, no, no!" he kept repeating. "No!"

"What the hell's the matter, Visocki?" I asked.

"They're waving the white flag," he groaned, throwing his gun to the ground.

We stood up. The firing had ceased. Up ahead, men with their hands upraised were slowly making their way to the waiting Germans. For the second time since we hit the line, a cold chill ran up my back. Surrender had been the furthest thought from my mind. Never did I think that I would ever fall into enemy hands. Somehow, though, I believed that it must have been in the back of my mind all the time. Then, a different feeling came over me, a feeling of relief, I think it was. Under the circumstances, it was the only way out. An attempt to fight in that draw would have massacred us all. As it was, we were at least alive. Visocki wanted to go back, but in the end, he relented.

And so Visocki, Charron, Durbin, and I followed the mob. First, however, there was the equipment to destroy. Everyone was busy destroying their weapons with relish. Rifle stocks were being smashed over machine gun jackets. Bolts were stripped and tossed in all directions. "Four hundred" mortar sights were smashed to bits. I field-stripped my own pistol completely and tossed the parts in a half-dozen directions. The ammunition I tossed into the waters. Monroe put an end to our machine gun's serviceability by distorting the sight leaf, smashing the water jacket and removing the bolt. Brand new and having fired about 150 rounds of ammunition, it was now destroyed. Somehow, this business of destroying had become great fun. Everyone was having such a good time! This was something that probably everyone in the army had wanted to do at some time or another. We were doing it now. Such gruesome fun!

Then we remembered the corned beef. With the aid of a bayonet, Monroe tore a hole in the top of a can and each of us took a handful of meat to be eaten before we reached the waiting Germans. It was when we reached the Germans that I realized how close we had come to total annihilation. One fellow was so close he could have rolled a grenade down on us. Why they chose to play with us in that draw, I will never know, but I am grateful.

We reached the first German, and he gave us a swift search of our pockets. Satisfied that we were hiding nothing, he moved us on to where a column of threes was already forming. Again we were searched. It was now that I decided to eat my can of beans before the Germans had a chance to take it from me. The Germans, however, were not as unscrupulous as we had expected them to be. A few of the men were stripped of their watches or other valuables, but the majority were allowed to keep them, particularly if the Germans found that we weren't trying to hide anything. One German, in fact, was giving cigarettes away to those who had none. He had found an entire carton which someone had thrown away thinking that the Germans would take them from us anyway.

"Hold onto them," he told us through an interpreter. "You're going to be begging for them someday." Now there was a man who knew what he was talking about.

It took the Germans over an hour to gather us together. We were many, and eventually the column broadened to five rows. Ready, they started marching us down the road, a tank leading the way.

It was now that we saw what we had been up against. The roads were crammed with machinery and vehicles that were moving up to the front. Tanks, trucks, and horse-drawn carts were lined up along one side for a mile or two. So we were going to attack this place and take it over, just like that, with no artillery support or even mortar support. It was going to be a cinch! What a farce. Yet despite the display of might, we realized that in comparison, the Germans were pitifully weak. One good strafing and all those horse-drawn vehicles would have rotted on that damn road.

In our march into town, we saw the tragedy that befell many of our own men in the initial day of battle when hell first burst loose in that town. Bodies of Americans, their combat shoes removed by the Germans for their own use, lay in ditches or beside overturned, charred vehicles. They were already, in turn, a moldy green, much as the dead German in front of Hilliard's dugout. They were as stiff and lifeless as the bodies in a wax museum. I saw one fellow with a bullet through his temple, his eyes nearly popped out of his head. Bob and Grube and Sheppard passed through my mind, and I hoped that they were not among the dead. It was pitiful. This was the real tragedy of wars. Everyone of these people was somebody's son, many were somebody's husband, maybe somebody's father. I even felt sorry for the Germans now. Why can't a weapon be devised that will not kill, but merely put the enemy to sleep? In fact, why wars?

IX

"It Was a Quiet Sector . . ."

I never did know the exact details of what happened to the 106th Division during and after our capture. I learned something of the story sometime after liberation in a syndicated article that I came across in the *Shreveport* (LA) *Times*. Among the things that surprised me was that the 106th had been highly praised by both the press and Secretary of War Stimson. The following is the article, written by E.D. Ball of the *Patterson Press,* entitled "It Was a Quiet Sector—They Went Down Fighting." Other newspapers had similar titles. My comments, when necessary, can be found parenthetically noted.

With the 106th Division in Belgium, Jan. 21 (AP)—
It was a quiet sector they handed the 106th Infantry Division, fresh to the front and raring to go on December 11 (1944).
The quiet ended in a shattering eruption of fire and steel five days later; in two days (actually three—SWR) two regiments and supporting artillery and armor of the Golden Lion Division were wiped out.
In those two days the men of two regiments were engulfed by the overwhelming weight of Field Marshall von Runstead's breakthrough spearhead. They went down fighting.
Only a handful came back from the 422 Regiment and the 423d. This little group, less than 300, pitched in and helped the remaining regiment, the 424th, so make gallant delaying stands before and behind St. Vith.
(Secretary Stimson announced that the 106th suffered 8,663 casualties in the German offensive including 416 killed and 1,246 wounded. He said that most of the division's 7,000 missing men were presumed to be prisoners.)
The story of the 106th started in the foggy dawn on December 16 as they occupied positions in and around the Schnee Eifel, a

rocky wooded ridge 10 miles long and two miles wide astride the Sigfried Line. The division was spread out pitifully along a 27-mile front.

Ironically, the 106th at this time was in almost the identical defensive position to that which it had held during Tennessee maneuvers in March '44 when it did so well the referee had to call time.

The attack started at 5:50 A.M. on the 16th with a tremendous artillery barrage against the 106th line which curved northward from the center of the Schnee Eifel to a sector held by the 4th Cavalry Group, an armoured outfit attached to the infantry. Then the barrage moved across a field artillery battalion, also attached. By 6:20 A.M. more than a hundred rounds had landed among the artillery men.

The Germans, meanwhile, switched on dozens of flashlights to introduce a ghostly and fantastic note. (Apparently, we were not subjected to this grotesque display as we saw no lights. Perhaps they never got close enough for us to see them or perhaps they lit up another sector—SWR.) Their scheme was for the lights to bounce off the low-hanging clouds and light up the American positions while the Germans advanced unseen through the shadows. It failed to work, however.

Five minutes after the shelling started, the Germans opened up against St. Vith itself. The civilians, most of whom pretended to be friendly but actually were pro-Nazi, were all in the cellars when the firing started. They popped out again when the last shell fell at 2:00 P.M. Americans later captured a radio receiver by which the Germans had notified the civilians of the impending shelling.

The Germans turned their guns then on the 422nd and 423rd and followed with Infantry and Tank assaults. By daybreak of December 17, the Germans had thrown two divisions into the front and by mid-morning enemy columns were swarming round the Schnee. They swarmed the 422nd and 423rd Regiments and the 424th was forced to withdraw.

All the time, until radio contact was lost, the two regiments continued to send reports of the fighting. They were routine in nature but they all added up to disaster. There was no sign however, that the men realized this or were overly concerned. (Note this last statement—SWR).

At 3:35 P.M. on December 18th, the radio sputtered that all units of the two regiments were in need of ammunition, food, and water. Parachuting supplies was out of the question because of the fog.

The last message came through the 422nd at 4:00 P.M. that day and the 423rd at 6:00 P.M. They were addressed to Lt. Col. Earle B. Williams, Louisville, KT, Division Signal Officer, and were signed by sergeants who were in charge of the radio team.

Both messages were in code and identical—"We are now destroying our equipment." That was all. Presumably, most of the two regiments were taken prisoner. (Obviously, the "destroying our equipment" was probably done by some units that were closer to the Germans than we were. We did not destroy our equipment until the 19th a day later—SWR)

Sorely exhausted and badly depleted, the 106th pulled back to reorganize on December 23, but the next day they were thrown into the line and helped halt the Germans finally on the north side of the salient between Stavelot and Manhay. (By this time Major General Alan Jones, our Division Commander, was no longer in charge of the 106th Division. He had been relieved on December 22 and, a few hours later, suffered a severe heart attack—SWR)

When Major General Alan W. Jones activated the 106th in March, 1943, he told the division "You're brand new—you have no past history to live up to and no past sins to live down."

They still have nothing to live down and much to be proud of, those men who got caught in one of the war's major battles before they had done more than night patrols . . .

Also of interest in connection with the 106th is the fate of St. Vith which was division headquarters at the time of the attack. Another article from the *Shreveport Times* describes the cataclysmic ruin of that little town during the German shelling and later during the American siege. It is entitled "Steam Shovels Used to Dig Out the Dead." Note the difference of opinion between Lewis Hawkins, who wrote this article, and Ed Ball, who wrote "Quiet Sector . . .", with respect to the feelings of the population of St. Vith.

St. Vith, Belgium.

Steam shovels are digging out St. Vith's dead today, six weeks after the war plowed them under and nobody knows how many bodies will be found or can say what is ahead for this once pretty little marked city.

Capriciously, the war thrice passed through St. Vith leaving it almost unharmed and then ironically crushed it with a finality ever seen in this area of destruction.

Here is what happened to St. Vith which had 3,500 inhabitants and the misfortune to be the hub of six major highways.

When the Germans recaptured the town December 22, the Americans were not strong enough to make a real battle, and war again touched lightly though the population had shrunk still more as officials and others had been helpful to the Allies fled westward.

The first warning of doom came on December 24 when medium bombers of the US 9th Air Force poured about 350 tons on the town's 350 to 400 buildings.

On Christmas the 8th Air Forces' Flying Fortress and Liberators, striking at the heart of the road net, dumped another 80 tons the following day and the RAF cascaded 1,130 tons in an assault, which, comparatively, was more than two times as heavy as the worst blow over London.

The first twenty-four hours of digging only yielded fifty bodies but there were many blocks yet to be churned over. So thorough was the destruction that only 9 houses remained habitable. About 80% of the remainder were leveled or completely smashed—

Finally, several books have been written about the "Battle of the Bulge" in which the story of the 106th Division is carefully dissected. I find that *A Time for Trumpets* (Morrow, 1985) by Charles B. MacDonald is a particularly thorough one. Mr. MacDonald wrote three of the U.S. Army's official histories and retired as Deputy Chief Historian of the U.S. Army. Chapter Sixteen, "The Defense of St. Vith," and other chapters in particular describe the fate of the 106th Division. Another is *Decision at St. Vith* by Charles Whiting (Ballantine Books, 1969), only in paperback but thorough nevertheless.

The only thing unanswered by all these books is, "What were we doing there in the first place?"

X
German Math: 40/8 = 60

It was a good forty-five minutes before we entered the town of Schoenberg. There the Germans led us into a large stable where we waited until they made up their minds what to do with us. Of course, the usual warning came first: "Don't try to escape." We were told, "If one escapes, twenty get shot!" The words were cold and distinct. We understood them well, though we didn't believe they would carry them out. They might try it on the Russians, we thought (smugly), but we were Americans. Nevertheless, no one tried to escape.

We remained in that barn for at least an hour. Then we were lined up again, recounted and re-searched, and when they were finally satisfied, they started marching us down the road, a small detachment of men leading the way. As we walked down the narrow street, I looked at the sneering population that came out to see us and couldn't help having some contempt for them. They were the same type of people that had smiled and seemed so friendly toward us at St. Vith as we moved up to the front. Now they laughed and sneered at us with such zest that I believe they thought they had won the war. But beneath our grim expressions, we were laughing too. At least we knew that we were going to have the last laugh—those of us who survived.

We marched that day until we thought we would march forever. We were tired, cold, and hungry. Ninety percent of us, including me, were suffering from frozen feet, and every step threatened to be our last.

We found our guards to be fairly decent fellows. We were given frequent breaks during the march, which was a big help and relief for our feet. They were talkative too. Most of them were Austrians or Russians who had been forced to bear arms, and there was a tone of resignation and weariness in their voices. Many of them hadn't been home for four years. When someone asked how long the war was going to last, they told us four to six months. We told them it might be quicker than that but they were skeptical while, at the same time, expressing their desire that it should end the next day. "Then we can all go home," one fellow told us.

Darkness came over us, and still we marched. Up and down hills, through battered towns and villages. All along we found that the Germans had been preparing. Tank traps had been built and those familiar V-shaped fox holes the Germans used were scattered over the fields and along the roads. It was obvious that the Germans were expecting the Americans and their allies, sooner or later.

Finally, tired, cold, and hungry, we arrived at our primary destination, the fortress town of Prüm. We had walked something short of twenty-six kilometers, or about 12 miles. On entering the town, we saw a large barn burning furiously; curiously no one was trying to put the fire out. The rest of the town lay in a heap of rubble. Many of the buildings were down and shattered with the remains of windows scattered along the streets. We were led through some winding streets and finally entered a square where stood an abandoned government building.

This was to be our shelter until morning. It was dark inside and difficult to see where anything was. There was, actually, very little. The second floor was still there but the planks had been torn loose by the bombings. I didn't know how that floor did not collapse with the weight of so many men on it, but I don't think anyone particularly cared. I found a bench to lie on, but as that became uncomfortable, I eventually slid to the floor with the rest of the men.

It was cold that night. I could feel the chill through my army overcoat. We slept soundly despite the temperature, and when I awoke the next morning, everyone was cuddled closely together along the walls and the floor. With the first rays of dawn, the men awoke and soon the place was buzzing with chatter. Everyone was eagerly looking forward to be fed. Many had not eaten for two days.

Food never came. Some civilians brought bread, but they were bartered by those who were lucky enough to have cigarettes. Had it not been for Lt. Knecht, I'd never have known what the bread even looked like. He had managed to buy a loaf, and despite his own hunger, he gave everyone in the platoon at least two good-sized bites. He even went out of his way to find those he could not locate immediately. This little incident convinced me that Lt. Knecht was really "one of the boys." I digested my share of the bread with relish. It was black, heavy, and sour, but I enjoyed it. I was hungry! Later, the Germans brought some water, which was a great relief for our mounting thirst.

Meanwhile, crap games started in all corners of the building. It seemed to me that no matter where a group of GIs get together, regardless of the situation or terrain, a crap game is imminent. With the few hundred francs I had left (the Germans didn't take it), I became involved in one. At first I was doing fine, but no sooner had I eaten my bread when my luck broke, and I was broke.

At about 10 A.M., the Germans ordered us outside to get ready to resume the march. It took them at least an hour to form us in columns of fives and count us again. Our column stretched back to what appeared to be at least 200 rows. It surprised me, for I didn't realize that there were so many of us. Others had joined us during the night. While we waited outside, shivering, I had a chance to look around. In the daylight, I could see that the town was in utter ruin and almost completely deserted. The Adolf Hitler Platz, where we were standing, looked like it may have been an impressive place at one time, but it was pretty much of a mess now. As for people, there just didn't seem to be any. Once, a small band of men came down the street, picks and shovels in hand. Obviously most of these "civilian volunteers" were digging the defenses in the hills surrounding the town.

And those hills were high! Prüm is situated deep in a valley, or pocket, that is formed by these hills. We found that out when we finally marched out of the town on our way to Gerolstein. Up and up we climbed as the road wound endlessly on top of these hills. Soon we tired and we hadn't even started. Once we arrived at the top, however, we found the road a bit smoother.

There was nothing, however, to stifle our hunger, which was becoming increasingly worse as we went along. The Germans promised us food when we got to Gerolstein, but when we asked how much further it was, they would answer, ten kilometers. Yet after every ten kilometers, it was another ten kilometers until we thought they would march us forever, or at least until all of us dropped from exhaustion or starvation. What was of some help were patches of sugar beets along the road. We raided every patch, eating anything we could find: beets, frozen potatoes, and roots. The Germans tried to put a stop to this but when we arrived at a cabbage patch just outside a small town, they found they could not control us. As a result, we stopped here for a while.

It was here that a German officer strode up with a movie camera and began taking pictures of us as we lay wearily on the road, munching on some turnips. Most of us turned away. Some snarled. The officer became angry and demanded that the men show their faces. It was a break for Nazi propaganda, which had become quite nil by now after so many months of retreats, defeats, and disasters. Showing the Americans at their worst would bolster the morale at the home front, at least for a little while.

And still we walked. Where was Gerolstein? "Ten more kilometers," said the German guard. I wondered if there was such a place. Finally, Gerolstein became a reality. A road sign read, "Gerolstein, 3 K", and soon we saw the town with its railroad yards and its singular pillarlike cliff in back of it. Here we would get rest and food, we hoped.

A large abandoned warehouse was our destination. We were gathered in a large yard in back of it, lined up in rows of five, and led into a warehouse one by one. At the door, we were handed our first food in two days: a box of kamradsbrodt, which were German field rations, and a cup of German coffee, which was splashed into our helmets.

If you've ever tasted matzos, then you've tasted kamradsbrodt, for these German rations were nothing more than hardened matzos packed in a cardboard box, four in a box. If you've ever tasted dishwater (probably not, unless you were a prisoner of war), then you've tasted what the Germans called coffee, for this erzatz blend of ground chicory, wood chips, and just plain dirt, had no more of a coffee taste than beach sand has. All in all, the meal was thoroughly distasteful, but I ate it, American style, dunking my komradsbrodt in the coffee. We were all quite hungry, and I'm afraid we would have eaten worse had they given it to us.

We all went to sleep that night, tired, weak, still hungry, in the filth and stench of that abandoned warehouse. It was stuffy and crowded, difficult to breathe in there. While most of the men made their beds on the floor of the warehouse. I found mine in a large bin, four tiers high. There, cramped as I was, and almost suffocating from the lack of fresh air, I nevertheless fell into a deep, reposing sleep.

In the morning, I woke up quite early only to find that everyone else was awake too. Everyone had eagerly awaited daybreak when the Germans might let us outside to get some air and some food, which they had promised us. Though we were expecting nothing more than another box of komradsbrodt, we were already looking forward to the distribution of this particular food, tasteless as it was.

The food finally came after we had lingered in the yard for some five or six hours. It turned out better than we expected. Instead of kamradsbrodt, we received two bags of hard biscuits, each bag containing about thirty biscuits. With it, we received a can of cheese which was to be distributed among six men. The hardtack turned out to be considerably better eating, and the cheese, greasy as it was, added a fair taste to what would have been basic crackers and water meal. The biscuits, when swallowed with water, expanded so that one bag was enough to satisfy one's stomach, for a while at least. When they ran out of crackers (or biscuits) they began giving out bread, seven men to a loaf.

Meanwhile, other prisoners were pouring in. Some had arrived during the night. Familiar faces appeared, among them Sgt. Lupo's, Platoon sergeant of the First Platoon, who was captured with his section intact. His First Section, however, was missing. What had happened to Adams, Strickland, Wattom, and the latter two squads nobody knew. The drivers were also missing, and no one knew about them.

By four o'clock, the Germans began marching us to the railroad yard, which we were to be transported to our prison camp. So many prisoners had been rounded up that the column of fives had grown to an endless procession of GIs, the end of which I never saw. I got the impression that the entire First Army had been captured.

At the station where the railroad cars were waiting, we were thrown into cattle cars, sixty men to a car, which allowed for very little living space. We were fortunate, I found out later, as compared to others who were crowded, like the literal sardines, eighty to a car. And then began a journey which I will remember as long as there are boxcars in the world: our five days and four nights in a German boxcar.

Technically, the car we were in was an Italian boxcar, recruited for use on the German rails. Normally, it held forty men or eight horses. It was made of strong steel, which I later came to appreciate, and had two double doors on each side. Luckily, each door had a small covered window which could be kept open while the train was in motion and the guards couldn't see it. This promised to be our saving grace, for without them, we would have died of the stench of our own waste. With the windows open we could relieve ourself in our helmets and throw the waste though the opening. Without them, we probably would have urinated or defecated all over each other and no doubt many of us would have collapsed from suffociation.

We were lucky, too, in another respect. Of the sixty men in our boxcar, fifty-eight were from our own company. Of the other two, one was a small, frightened Jewish boy from the 423rd and the other was an intensely religious young man who seemed to resent any argument or derogatory use of words during the trip, which took place often. Virtually, we were all D Company men who thought we could get along better among ourselves. I would venture to guess that we did more arguing knowing each other than if we were absolute strangers. Sergeants were cursing privates; privates were cursing sergeants; everybody was cursing anybody at the slightest provocation.

The train finally started out of the station, and we were on our way, destination unknown. However, we didn't expect to spend any more than a day or two in the boxcar, so unawares were we of our air force's efficiency on matters of railroads. It was dark now, and after situating ourselves as best we could, we tried to get some sleep. There was not enough room for everyone to lie down and there was considerable grumbling that night, not only from those who were forced to stand, but also by those on the floor who, as they tossed and turned during the night, found themselves on top or below them or with one leg on somebody's stomach or a foot in somebody's face. Indignant remarks also came from those who could not toss or turn at all and woke up with their legs semiparalyzed, their backs aching, or their feet frozen, for at night, the boxcar was a giant refrigerator with ice forming over the entire walls of the car. My feet were swollen and aching to begin with, but when morning came, I thought they would fall off, or, worse yet, they would have to be amputated someday.

The next morning, we found ourselves further in Germany, though not very deep. I don't think we had traveled twenty kilometers. No sooner did the train move a few kilometers, when the train stopped for a few hours. We opened the window to get some fresh air, and Norman Martin, who mixed his German with his Yiddish, asked one of the guards why he had stopped.

"Engine trouble," was the reply.

"Better ask him when we're going to get something to eat," someone suggested. We were hungry again, and I had finished my biscuits during the night. Martin put the question.

"*Brot?*" exclaimed the German. "You just ate!"

This was a little discouraging, and we wondered when they were going to feed us again.

All the way, the train had made little progress. We moved for a few kilometers and then stopped again. Meanwhile, we had nothing else to do but talk, shoot crap, and play cards.

Night came on again. We now began to dread these long, dark, and restless hours. This time we made an attempt to get everyone on the floor, but within an hour, the grumbling and cursing began again, at an even more furious tempo than the night before.

The hours passed slowly. The night was cold and uncomfortable. I found a better position in the car this time and suffered less than I did the night before. Within the cold confines of the car, we "sweated out" the morning.

Morning finally came, and the first thing we did was to ask for "*brot* and *wasser.*" "Also," explained Martin, "*wir muss scheissen,*" for some were already suffering from the GI trots. Two sergeants had already embarrassingly deposited their guts in their pants.

"*Ja, ja, ja,*" assured us the German. "*Brot, wasser, scheissen.*"

All morning we waited, and all morning we pestered them. Finally, at about 2:00 P.M., the Germans brought us some *wasser* in buckets and at about 5:00 P.M., they came out with the *brot.* They would not permit us to get out of the boxcar, however, for *scheissen.* We were given ten loaves, each loaf to be divided among six men, and half a helmut full of spread, which may have been molasses. The bread we ate with the depravity of hungry beasts. Some, at first, found the black bread difficult to swallow. I didn't find it as bad as it looked, and ate it all. Our stomachs comparatively full, the situation took on a brighter aspect, and though we dreaded the night that was closing in on us, we were a bit more cheerful. This cheeriness, however, was to be supplanted a few minutes later by an atmosphere of complete horror, a horror that none of us on that train will ever forget.

Our train stopped on the main track just outside of the town of Lindberg, which, I later learned, had many POW camps situated nearby. We had no sooner finished our bread when the air alert sounded. We had heard several before, but the planes generally passed overhead on their way to central Germany. This time, however, they weren't going any further than Lindberg. Within minutes, colored flares began dropping from the sky, lighting the ground like a movie set. Then it seemed that the planes were diving at us, with bombs falling, creating terrific explosions that occurred so close, they rocked the boxcar.

Within a split second everyone dropped to the floor. Some were screaming, others were crying; panicky ones wanted to jump from the window and run for safety, somewhere. Actually we were safer in the boxcar than we might have been outside; at least we had a steel compartment protecting us from flying shrapnel. One fellow was yelling "Shoot me! Shoot me," and he was dragged to the floor. Everyone was as close to the floor as they could possibly get, even those who could not find room during the night found it now. Somebody was yelling, "Get off me!" Another was begging someone to let him hide beneath him. "I'll get hit on top of you," he cried. Then the car became deadly quiet. I doubt whether anyone dared breathe aloud.

There were many prayers said that evening. Some were earnest, well said prayers; others were the mere rambling of men too scared to know what they were saying. It's amazing how, in the face of death, man's thought turned to God in search of comfort and forgiveness. I suppose, during those few horrible moments, many repented every sin they had ever committed.

Only one sour note was heard. While men, like Olecki, were exhorting us to keep praying, one, JT, would shout "Where's prayin' gonna get ya." They may have been the words of someone who had gone hysterical, or he may have meant it. In any case, they were loudly resented. He was told to keep his mouth shut several times and had everyone not been so busy hugging the floor, he might have been told more forcefully.

We lay there, cuddled together for some time. I must have died a thousand deaths and am not ashamed to admit it. I held my breath and shut my eyes with every wail of falling bombs and prayed and prayed and prayed. One bomb blew the window open. Hysteria was loose again, the fear of shrapnel coming through the window frightened us. It was York who finally shut the window and saved us, at least from ourselves. Another bomb came close enough to jar the doors loose from its slide. Through the space created between the door and the slide I could see flares fall while great flashes of red lit the entire landscape around us.

Finally, after ten frightening minutes—that's all it lasted—the planes departed. Yet we dared not move. We knew that the planes usually came in waves. This was the first wave, and we expected the second to be on top of us any minute.

But the second wave never came, and after about fifteen or twenty minutes the all-clear signal sounded, and we had enough to rise from the floor and open the windows. The guards, who had scattered in all directions, were back now. Martin asked what damage was caused, but he was either too frightened, too busy, or just didn't care to answer him.

That night we went to sleep, hoping that we would never have a similar experience again, and that they would get us to our camp as soon as possible. Again, we took our positions on the floor, soon to resume our grumbling.

The next morning we were able to learn something of the bombing the night before. The planes, the German told us, were British. The objective was a rail junction a quarter of a mile ahead of us. The damage they had caused was considerable. The tracks had been destroyed at this point, and a deep cavity was made in the ground necessitating that it be built up again. Workmen were already at it, he told us, rather proud of their efficiency. The tracks weren't the only installation hit. A water main had burst also. Worst of all, a POW barracks had been hit. The Germans placed these barracks too close to the railroad so that hitting the barracks was almost inevitable if the railroad was the target. (I later learned that this barrack contained American officers, several of which were killed. Rumor also had it that one of our boxcars had suffered injury too, but that was never established.)

Before long, our thoughts were again turned to brot, Wasser, and Scheissen. It had been at least three days now since most of us had moved our bowels. For me it had been six, and still, when they finally let us out, one car at a time. I had neither the ambition nor the energy, not even the urge, to relieve myself. This, I realized, was not a healthy situation, yet actually, I had very little to relieve; two scanty "antipastos" in five days was hardly enough to get my stomach excited.

They accommodated with wasser too, but we had to pay for it, this time with cigarettes, and for each trip they made, it cost us from five to ten cigarettes.

The brot came too, at about five that evening. First it was two loaves for the whole car. At this, we were very disappointed, though we considered ourselves lucky to get even that, especially since we had eaten the day before. We cut the loaves up into thirty chunks apiece, each man receiving a mouthful. But this was Christmas Eve, and although it wasn't the Christmas spirit that moved them, they gave us ten more loaves an hour later, and some molasses too.

Finally, there was a jerk, and the train began to move, much to our relief.

When we finished eating our precious black bread, we began to sing Christmas carols. It wasn't long, however, before our voices trailed away and our thoughts turned to home. As I lay there, I could see my mother cooking her Christmas Eve meal. It was a meatless meal, as was customary in Catholic Italian families, and much looked forward to with its great variety of fish, not the least of which was fried octopus. I could see her preparing her wonderful pastries for the Christmas meal. Then, too, I could see her going to midnight Mass with my sister. I would be missed this year, just as I was missed the year before, but there would be a big difference between this Christmas and the last one back home. I prayed that my family would be spared these first telegrams until at least the new year.

I saw my father that night. My thoughts wandered way back to when my father was still putting me to sleep in his arms. I must have been three, maybe four, but I remembered my fooling him one night and how he had laughed when he discovered my trick. And later, when my mother and I would go to Midnight Mass, my father used to go to sleep at the table at home. And how surprised he looked when we returned and found that Santa Claus had already been there. "My God!" he would say, keeping a perfectly straight face. "He must have come while I was asleep!"

"But from where?" my mother would ask.

"Down the chimney," my father replied, "or maybe through the bathroom window."

I remembered, too, that morning of December 8, 1943, when I left for Camp Upton, Long Island. I was eager, excited, and couldn't wait to get underway. I didn't know what I was getting into, but my father did. Perhaps he was thinking of his own World War I days when he kissed me good-bye. Perhaps he recalled his own experiences in the battles of the Marne and Argonne (He had been wounded just above the heart by two ricocheting machine gun bullets). I saw tears come out of his eyes for the first time in my life.

I remembered my sister too. She was eleven years old. Somehow, I felt that I had never spent enough time with her. Things would change when I got back home, if I ever got back.

Other things passed through my mind, and there were moments when I wanted to cry but didn't. At last, my eyes grew heavy and I fell asleep. But just before I did, I heard a voice break the silence. "Move over, you sonofabitch," it said. The grumblers were grumbling, even on Christmas Eve.

I awoke once during the night. This time, instead of standing still or hardly moving as we usually did, the train was traveling at a terrific speed, such speed, in fact, that I wondered whether the Germans hadn't thrown the throttle wide open, deserted the train, and let the engine run on a track that probably led to the edge of a cliff. It wasn't a pleasant thought, and I didn't believe it, but the train then slowed down for a moment, and I was relieved, whereupon I fell asleep again.

Morning came once again, and we were still moving, slowly again. It was a beautiful Christmas morning. The sun was the strongest it had been in weeks. It was an ideal morning for bombing. Just another day for the Germans, I thought, but even the beauty of the day couldn't hide the scene of utter destruction that we saw when we passed through Coblenz.

We passed through Coblenz at about nine that morning. Never had I seen such destruction anywhere. Coblenz had been flattened, leveled to the ground by the incessasnt bombing of our B-25s. Nowhere could I find a building that could boast of four walls and a ceiling. One wall, half a wall, no wall remained of structures that were probably once proud government buildings, giant factories, and peaceful dwellings. All that was left was rubble. In contrast, across the river, there was no destruction.

At this point, I wish to point out that we now held the dubious honor of being the first American unit to cross the Rhine. After all, hadn't they captured the entire battalion, the entire regiment, just about the entire division? As one fellow put it, we were just being smuggled in.

The train rolled on. We sidetracked twice, then came to a railroad junction, and we were very near our destination. At about 2:00 P.M. we arrived. The sign at the station read: "BAD ORB."

XI

Stamlager IX B

The boxcar was filled with great expectations. Food, a bed, and warmth were possibly close at hand, we thought. Within a few moments, we were ordered out of the boxcars, one car at a time, and told to form a column of fives. I had been so cramped for the past five days that I could barely stand up. When we were formed and counted, they began marching us from the station, and at last, we were on the last lap of our journey, at least for now.

"*Wiefiel* kilometers?" we asked, for we were hardly in any shape for walking. Not only were we weak from lack of food and the curse of diarrhea, but most of us, having resigned ourselves to our little corner in the boxcar, sitting in the same spot for days at a time, had become almost paralyzed. So unstable were my legs that I nearly collapsed when I jumped from the train.

"*Fünf* kilometer," replied the guard, and he raised his five fingers to indicate the number.

We had heard that story before, but surprisingly, the Germans were telling us the truth this time. It was five kilometers, about three miles. But they were the longest five kilometers that we had ever marched.

We were walked through the middle of town, an inevitability that would not be avoided, even though there might have been a more direct route to the camp. After all, we were great morale builders for the Germans. We looked so tired, weary, and beaten that they must have thought the war was going to end within weeks, in their favor. If they did, though, they didn't show it. Actually, there seemed to be little enthusiasm for the show.

They stood along the streets in their holiday best, looking at us with glum faces, chatting among themselves. It seemed as though they were looking at us more out of curiosity than anything else.

Bad Orb apparently had not been hit too hard by the war. Our own bombers had not molested it in any way. There wasn't a house that was damaged, and even the railroad was spared, all possibly because of the prison nearby. The more probable reason was that there were no factories there other than a bread mill. The town itself was beautiful and spotless. All the buildings were typical two-story family dwellings with snow-covered gardens in front and back of the houses. It struck me that this place was a health resort, and subsequently I was to find that I was right. It was high up in the mountains, and the air was fresh and clean.

The one road leading to the camp began on a normal enough level, but before we had walked one kilometer, it was winding through the hills at a fairly stiff incline. This was what made the five kilometers seem like twenty. As we hiked our way up, the town disappeared behind us. The journey became increasingly difficult, until many of us had to sit down from sheer exhaustion. By the time we had walked these five kilometers, we had three breaks. At one point, a familiar sign appeared by the last house. It read, "Drink Coca Cola." *Oh, for a bottle of that now,* I thought to myself. The thought was not original. Everyone else was thinking the same thing.

We finally reached the camp. It took the Germans an hour to get us in the formation that they wanted, the officers in one group, the noncoms in another, and the privates in a third group. This done, they searched us once more. Everything I possessed was in my helmet: a razor, complete with twenty blades, my glasses, a pen, some paper, and just plain junk. The guard, who wasn't too swift, ignored the razor, the glasses, and the pen, my most worthy possessions. Then he spotted the old pencils. He picked them up, looked at them, poked the German next to him and said *"Bleistift,"* as if to ask whether I should be allowed to keep them. The other guard looked at him and waved his hand as if to say, "Ja, let him keep the damn things. What are you bothering me for?" Thus, I was allowed to pass. In retrospect, this was an important moment for me, for had the pencils been taken (the pen had no ink) I might not have written essential parts of this manuscript. When they finished searching us, we were marched to our barracks. The noncommissioned officers were placed in one barrack, marked 43; the officers, led by Col. Thompson of the 3rd Battalion, were placed in the first half of barrack 42, and five hundred of us privates and Pfc's were placed in barrack 44. The remainder of the privates were placed in a barrack nearby.

It was dark now, and finding empty bunks was difficult. However, about a dozen of us from D Company managed to find a vacant spot. The Germans had promised us food. It was Christmas, they told us, "but don't expect turkey." In a little while Christmas dinner was brought in. It consisted of three large barrels and two small buckets of soup. The soup appeared to be made of greens that ordinarily only the cows would eat. Somewhere, hidden among the greens, were some potatoes. They were, however, very rare, and not everyone saw one. Besides the soup, there was black bread, six men to a loaf again, with a slab of margarine. It was a sad meal, but beggars can't be choosers, and, as we soon found out, it was the "biggest" single meal we would have as prisoners of war. I was hungry and ate the bread and drank the soup. Others found the bread too heavy to swallow and the soup distasteful and threw it away. It would be the only food to be disposed of in that manner while we were at the Stamlager.

We went to sleep that night, two in a bunk, one because of the lack of bunks, and second, it was the best way to keep warm. There was no heat at all in the barracks that night, and the wind that blew in through the window near our bunk was terrific.

The bunks in the Stamlager were wooden structures, three high and two deep. Two rows of bunks formed a group of six, and between each group was a three-foot aisle with a shuttered window. There must have been about twenty-five groups on each side of the barrack. The barrack itself was divided by a washroom in the center, and running the length of the barrack was a twelve-foot passageway. Two wood stoves were located in each half barrack. At the far ends of the barrack was a room which served as a toilet. Each room contained a large tub for urine and a bare hole for turd.

Several of us occupied two of the groups. On one side of the aisle, on the top tier, and nearest the window, slept Charron and Durbin. Next to them slept Monroe, alone. Below him were Turongian and Rosenberg. Next to them were Brummer and me. Across the aisle were Ramsy and Brankin. On the third tier in the front bunk nearest our aisle, slept B.J. Vogel and next to him Hugh Griffin. The two merged forces at night but kept separate bunks during the day.

Brummer and I slept comfortably that night, at least as comfortably as two people in a wooden bed three feet wide and six feet long can be. We had mattresses, burlap bags filled with excelsior, but that didn't help much. One night's sleep, and it flattened out to such a degree that it was almost as hard as the boards beneath it. We would get used to that. Both of us had field jackets and overcoats, which gave us an advantage over some. Yuskie and Hammond had no overcoats, so we gave them our field jackets. All of us had sweaters.

We were awakened the following morning at about six by a German guard, a staff sergeant, who came in yelling "Cafe *Hollen!*" One of the fellows in our barracks named Warren knew German rather well (he had already assumed the role of interpreter and therefore command) and from him, we learned that the German wanted a detail to pick up our coffee, and presumably, breakfast. *Ah,* we thought, *coffee, bread, maybe cereal too.* Volunteers were sought and easily gathered, and the detail followed the guard to get breakfast.

When they returned we were sorely disappointed to find that one, there was no cereal; two, there was no bread; and three, there was no coffee, at least what we might call coffee. What we received wasn't even bad coffee. It was just plain hot water, blackened by boiling it with chicory and some erzatz blend. Furthermore, we learned that the food we had received the night before was not one full meal but an entire day's ration. In short, our ration was to be the hot water for breakfast (sometimes it would be called tea, depending on what it was made with (herbs or chickory), a canteen cup of soup (a half-liter), mostly greens for lunch (dinner) and a sixth of a loaf of black bread with perhaps a slab of margarine for supper. This was not a very hearty menu, to say the least.

That afternoon I learned that men can be pigs when they live like pigs. When the soup arrived and the barrels had been emptied, some of the boys (none of ours) rushed to the barrels, ran their filthy hands along the inside to gather anything that might have stuck to the barrels, and licked their hands and fingers of anything they had gathered. That evening at supper, ten loaves of bread were stolen so that sixty men went without bread.

The fault, of course, lay in the fact that there was no system by which each man could receive an equal share of the food. There was no way of stopping those who slid back into line for seconds while others had yet to get their soup. The bread was given out to men on their word that they had five men to share it with and no way of checking to find out whether he was doing this or not, or whether any man was receiving bread from two different sources. It became obvious that some system was necessary and even the guards realized this, for they threatened to let us go hungry altogether if everyone didn't get their share of food.

After two or three days of confusion and argument at chow time (breakfast wasn't considered) some brilliant person on the other side of the barracks suggested the simple idea of forming squads, a squad leader and five other squad members. In this manner, each squad would wait their turn for soup at lunch, and each squad leader would pick up the bread at suppertime. In this manner, no one could get more or less than their share.

It was a remarkable idea, and it worked. Everyone fell in with his own friends and one was appointed squadleader. Because there were too many of us for one squad, we divided into two squads. Brummer was elected as squadleader of one squad and I of the other. (Frankly, I never wanted the job, and as I found out later, never should have taken it.) Besides Brummer, his squad consisted of Charron, Durbin, Yuskie, Hammond, and Rosenberg. In mine were Turongian, Griffin, Ramsey, Monroe, and Brakin. B.J. Vogel had already joined another squad consisting of D Company men.

Following this arrangement, we only had minor troubles with the food except from a minority of trouble makers. Sometimes, one or two loaves of bread were found missing, and those who were stealing them were the very men we had appointed as cooks (or "servers"); the men who were giving out the marmalade, when there was any, and poured out the soup. We must have changed these "cooks" at least five times the first month at the Stamlager, and every time for the same reason. Not all of them stole bread, of course. One reason why the cooks were relieved of their jobs was because they would take their share (and often more) of the soup when the barrels were nearly empty, when the broth had been consumed, and the solids remained. This, we complained, was not right, even if they were cooks. Why should they get solids every day while we got broth. But every time we changed cooks for new ones, it was the same old story. It all ended, finally, when the Germans gave us our own kitchen. (Up until then, the French were cooking our food; our cooks merely picked it up in barrels and served it. For that, we called them "cooks," but that was the extent of their fame.) But even though the soup problem was fairly cleaned up, there would be another complaint, this one about the bread and how the cooks would keep the larger loaves for themselves or their friends. The poor cooks were attacked by everyone, until finally, those who weren't thrown out of their jobs, quit them in disgust.

There was another difficulty concerning the food. This applied to the eating utensils. There just weren't any. The first day we were forced to eat out of our helmets. Then the Germans gave us some mess kits, but many of these were either rusty or so filthy that many decided it would be better to continue eating out of their helmets. The food itself we were forced to eat with our hands. The Germans gave us no spoons, and we didn't have any. I remembered what someone told us in England: "No matter what happens, always have your mess kit with you!" (I wondered whether Lt. Hotaling still had his mess kit.) Some talented fellows carved wooden spoons for themselves with various small knives that the Germans let them keep. I eventually made one myself, and eating became much more pleasant. Even the food tasted better, for whatever compliment that may be. Sometime later the Germans issued about two dozen combination fork-and-spoons, which were given out to those who needed them badly because of trench mouth. I kept eating with my own spoon. I still have it, a souvenir of the appreciation of food, even though I developed the disease toward the end.

This prison camp, a *"stamlager"* in German, was numbered IXB. Actually, there were two Stamlager IXBs, the other being situated in Ziegenheim, about twenty miles away, which was where the noncommissioned officers were transported later. The camp dated back to the last World War, when it was a POW camp too. Following the war, it was converted to a children's camp. With the beginning of World War II, it was reconverted once again into a POW camp, this time for French, Russians, and Serbs. For us, it was supposed to be merely a "reception" center, a place from which we were to be sent to an established American camp. At the time of our arrival, there were some 8,000 prisoners, mostly French and Russian, some Serbs, and a few Italians. There had never been any Americans there before.

The camp itself was not very big. It was barely a half mile long and not much more than half a mile wide. Two barbed wire fences about three feet apart surrounded the camp with spools upon spools of barbed wire thrown between the fences for added confinement. The barracks, numbered up to 45, with latrines and kitchen included, stood close together, some fenced off from the others by the same barbed wire. Except for a few (40, 43, 44, 45, and 25, which was to become our hospital), they were made all of wood with ripped tin roofs. The others were made of concrete and stucco, which made them somewhat safer from strafing or bombing, though this factor of safety could hardly be a factor. Each barrack was divided into two sections, usually by a washroom which was used by both. At both ends of the stucco barracks were the latrines. They were to be used at night, but with the lack of illumination, the rooms were usually filthy with deposit in the mornings. Everyone who had to go put some distance between himself and the hole, assuming that the person before him had done the same thing.

On December 28, three days after we arrived at Bad Orb, the Germans decided that what we needed was a delousing and a shower. I remember the day because it was Turongian's birthday and we all thought what a wonderful birthday present it was. (As much as this was Turongian's birthday, this day was deeply mourned at my home. On that date, in 1908, a cataclysmic earthquake hit Messina, Italy. It killed over 80,000 people there and in surrounding towns, including my grandfather, an uncle, and an aunt. My mother, who was sleeping with my aunt, was buried for several hours before somebody spotted her pigtails under the rocks and dug her out. Then, in 1937, my grandmother died on that day at the age of seventy. But this was another year, and the big event was a delousing.)

To use an unoriginal pun, "We were lousy with lice." We had caught our first louse in the warehouse at Gerolstein, spread it on the train, and in the three days we had been in Bad Orb, had become so infested with them that we were scratching day and night. I even scratch now to think about it. The shower and a delousing, though it cleaned us temporarily, was of little help, for no sooner did we get back to the infested excelsior mattresses when we had become as "lousy" as we had been before.

At this point, I ruefully note that I was wearing a pair of OD pants and shirt that I had put on in Fairford on Thanksgiving Day and had not removed them at all from my body since we left France on December 8. Furthermore, I did not get to remove them again until our first delousing and our second delousing (March 28) when the Germans, anticipating the approach of our own troops, decided they had better give us another delousing. But the same clothes went back on again until two weeks later when the Americans were finally able to reclothe us entirely. Therefore, I wore the same clothes without having them washed once, except for two delousings, for nearly five months. I'm sorry to admit that I wore my underclothes for nearly as long.

Following our delousing, on that same day, we were called upon to fill out our registration cards. These were, however, not the cards that we were waiting to fill out, our Red Cross cards. These were German cards for German files, consisting of a series of eight questions. I remembered what we were told in England, "Name, rank, and serial number, and that's all!" As it turned out, however, most of us answered the questions, for there seemed to be nothing that asked for military information. It asked for name, rank, serial number, branch of service, mother's maiden name, and three others which I frankly don't remember. (Could one of them have to do with religion?) I was reluctant to answer the questions about branch of service and mother's maiden name, but everyone else did and so did I. For branch of service, they wanted to know if I was in the Infantry, Artillery, etc., but almost everyone answered U.S. Army and no more was said by the Germans.

Actually, there wasn't any military information they would have gained anyway. They had captured most of the 106th, a good part of the 28th, and a mixture of men from other divisions they were already familiar with. There was nothing they could have learned from us that they had not already learned at St. Vith, *or even further,* I thought to myself, wondering, how much further had the Germans gotten by now.

There were some, however, who had refused to give any information other than their name, rank, and serial number. B. J. Vogel and Hugh Griffin were two of them. BJ gave in because he was Jewish and didn't want to exacerbate the situation. Griffin, however, continued to refuse. The Germans, who were equally as stubborn and held the upper hand anyway, forced him to stand outside in the cold until he did as they wanted him to. After three or four hours, Griffin finally gave in, but still refused to give his home address. I asked him about it later that night.

"Griffin," I said, "why in hell did you want to freeze out there? Everyone else answered the questions, and your answers wouldn't have made any difference."

He looked at me and said, "A matter of principle, Raffa, a matter of principle."

The days passed, and by New Year's Eve, we had become accustomed to our surroundings, if not our hunger. That night I was especially hungry, for New Year's Eve was the night that we ate the most food and the most delicious pastries in the house. It was tradition, at my house, that everyone was to taste at least thirteen kinds of foods that night. We had fritters and cookies and pastries like cannoli, torrone, babas, fruit of all sorts, ranging from dry string figs and dates to apples, pears, and tangerines, and a half-dozen assortment of nuts. There would be wine and whiskey and vermouth, marsala, rasolio, creme di cacao, or anisette. After the feast, we would settle down to a game of poker or seven-and-a-half (the Italian twenty-one) or Sweep (the Italian casino), and after we were dead tired and our stomachs full, we went to bed for a few hours rest. I wondered what this New Year's Eve would be like back home. The food would be there, but the spirit would be something else.

On New Year's Day, the Germans finally decided that we were ready to fill out our Red Cross cards. We did this with great joy and expectation, and with a feeling of great relief. The Red Cross is one big hope in a prison camp. Not only would their packages now supplement our needs, but through the Red Cross, our relatives would learn of our capture, and even if it wasn't exactly good news they received, it would at least remove the doubt and anxiety that the MIA telegram was bound to create.

Through the Red Cross, we would be able to correspond with our folks back home, and they could send us packages of food, clothes, and basic necessitites. We knew, too, that it would bring Red Cross packages and emergency rations to our camp. Most of all, the Red Cross gave us a feeling of security, a sort of protection against maltreatment through the Geneva Convention. We learned later, however, that the Red Cross is not always as efficient as it tries to be, due to obstacles and circumstances that get in the way, impediments not of their own doing.

We had another treat coming to us that day, and it came at dinnertime. Instead of greens that had been our diet for the past seven days, the Germans fed us pea soup. This was really a treat as I had never had pea soup before, and it tasted far better than the greens despite their looking like a misty green broth. Every noon from then on, we would be eagerly looking forward to having pea soup, only to be disappointed to learn that we were to get it twice a week at the most.

The next day, Tuesday, the Germans had another surprise for us. Actually, it was something that they were obligated to do under the terms of the Geneva Convention (which they insisted they had never heard of). A form letter was distributed to each man on which he could write home. This was the first of two letters and four cards that we were allowed to write each month. I remember distinctly the gist of what I wrote in that letter. (Surprisingly, this arrived home, and before the MIA telegram.)

"Send me packages," I wrote, after assuring my folks of my safety, my "good health," and my "fair treatment." Then I went on to describe what I wanted. I had heard that packages sent from home through the Red Cross could not be more than seven pounds, so I was forced to limit myself in my request. I asked for food, of course, and sweets, and crackers, and pastry (it didn't seem to faze me that it would be hard as a rock when and if it got to me), and even for a package of Sen. I also asked for a small notebook and pencil and a pair of socks. "Then," I added, "if there are any vacant spots in the box, fill them up with jelly beans." In ending the letter, I tried to be funny, yet consoling, and wrote "so turn on the radio again, take off your black clothes, and go on eating your spaghetti like nothing happened, for I'll be home before you know it."

Needless to say, no packages ever arrived.

That I asked for paper and a pencil was relevant. I liked to write, some of it bad, but nevertheless, I enjoyed doing it. I began to realize now that I might as well do something to pass my time, for there was absolutely nothing to do between meals except talk, play cards, and sweat out the next meal. As the talk was always about food, there wasn't much future in it, and as rummy and hearts became quite boring after the first two hundred games (someone had a pack of cards that were all but faded by the time we were liberated), I decided to write a story. It had nothing whatsoever to do with the prison camp, although I jotted down incidents as they occurred. It was about a certain Dr. Ito and his magnificent mental tortures. (Somehow, my mind, even then, leaned to the macabre and sadistic.)

I started the story on December 28th, scribbling sentences on every scrap of paper I could dig up until it was nearly finished and I completely ran out of paper. I was stuck in the story with the mad doctor on the verge of killing off his wife. Everyone rejoiced at this. They were sick and tired of having me write all day, not because they didn't have anyone to play cards with, but because they were secretly jealous of me, who was able to occupy my time writing while they had nothing else to do but think and talk about food!

Then, one day I got lucky. A detail of one man was to be sent to the office to pick up toilet paper, and it was my turn to go. The paper I was given were old German files on one side of which were the records of men who passed through the camp and the other side being totally blank. I returned with the paper, but not before I slipped a batch of about one-half inches thick under my sweater. Thus, I was able to finish and recopy my story and write another one besides. I called it "The Case History of Dr. Ito." Further statistics on this literary gem of mine are:

completed January 20, 1945 (twenty-four days after I started it). Recopied February 4, 1945. Total number of words (I counted them carefully) 13,955. I have since recopied it and given it a professional touch, and it has yet to be rejected. (Naturally, since I have never offered it for publication to a breathless, waiting public.)

The days, amazingly enough, passed rather swiftly, though every day it was the same old thing, the same old grind. Day in and day out, "we went without the meat and cursed the bread," and all we could talk about was going home and eating food. Besides myself, the only writing anyone ever did was in creating huge menus that they were going to have or invent fantastic recipes that they were going to try, all of this when they got home. I was no exception. I was as hungry as the next guy, and many times I yearned for a plate full of macaroni and meatballs. I had my menu too. This one, I prepared for my first Sunday at home.

Breakfast: Tomato juice, 7 pancakes w/butter and syrup (I was careful not to exclude any details) 2 eggs over w/bacon, toast w/butter, jelly, and bananas, milk.

Dinner: (This was a big one). Oven baked macaroni with tomato sauce, meat balls, mozzarella cheese, sliced eggplant and grated cheese; Veal cutlets oven baked with sauce and mozzarella cheese; lettuce and tomatoes, stuffed eggplants, Italian bread, wine, coffee, Italian pastry of all varieties, demitasse.

Supper: Roast chicken w/sweet potatoes, Long Island potatoes, peas, onions, carrots, tomatoes, lettuce, and sliced cucumbers; Italian bread with provolone cheese; Italian pastries; jello w/bananas, ice cream (Neopolitan), demitasse.

Evening Snack: (I always had something before going to bed.) Apple pie, cake, jelly donuts, and milk. I even had a menu for between meals: Banana splits, jelly donuts, cookies, and candies, especially malt balls.

It was an enormous menu. In it I tried to squeeze most of my favorite dishes. Other, even larger, menus were created by

Hammond, who insisted he could eat at least thirty-five pancakes at one sitting. He was going to have that and *lots* of white bread with *lots* of peanut butter when he got home. It was preposterous, and at times, we made ourselves ravenously hungry talking about cinnamon buns, cream puffs, chocolate eclairs, and homemade fudge. "And just wait!" said Hammond, "when I get home, I don't care where we are, even if we have to camp in the park, I'm going to have my wife bring over a ninety-five-pound pig and we're going to have an old-fashioned barbeque with *aaaall* the meat you want!"

I promised the boys a real Italian spaghetti dinner.

Even more preposterous than the menus were the recipes that were created. Concoctions like chocolate plumb pie and prune custard pie suddenly sprang into existence, not to mention a variety of sherberts, marshmallow specials, candy cocktails, and peanut embrolios.

"Gowan," said the boisterous Hammond one day to one of the boys nearby. "There aint no such thing as prune custard pie. How can you make custard out of prunes!"

"Sure you can. I'll bet you can" was the curator's answer.

"Gowan," replied Hammond. The same argument flared up every day for the rest of our stay at the Stamlager. Even at night, if Hammond heard that same fellow talking about recipes, he would remark "Ha! Ha! That's the guy who's going to make prune custard pie!"

All this recipe business going on around me was too much for me to ignore. Eventually, I found myself copying recipes like mad and giving some of my own. I still have a small army address book in which I copied the recipes. They consist of well-known cakes, pies, and desserts, which I promised to try at home but never did, and a few fudge marshmallow mixtures. Others around me were rushing around like mad, collecting recipes, forming dishes from French cajun to Indian styles, scribbling menus of every kind, jotting down the names of important restaurants from Hollywood to New York and from Midvale to Chatham, places they were going to visit when they got home.

It was farcical, though actually a little sad. I doubt whether any of these people looked at these papers since their liberation. Yet that was the way of the Stamlager. Everywhere you went, the talk was Food! Food! Food!

It was about mid-January that our food situation improved, or at least got a little better. By this time, the Germans had let us have our own kitchen, where the soup was cooked by GIs who had previous experience in the army or as civilians. Actually, no one needed any experience to mix a soup that lacked variety and, often, taste. As for the coffee they made in the morning, it was little more than the process of boiling water with some er- zatz sediment, all of which required no experts with letters of introduction. As it was, however, everyone received more soup and everyone received their share of the "solids," for the cooks were impartial in giving their one liter per man. After all, their stomachs were full at night when they fried themselves some of the horse meat they had not thrown into the pot. The process of making food too was cleaner. The French, in filling the barrels of food that were sent to us when we first got there, stepped right into the immense vats with some hip boots and practically bathed themselves in it while they shoveled some of the solids into the barrels. I suppose that this didn't do more harm than eating out of the our filthy mess kits. But the very thought of not having the Frenchmen step all over it gave the food a bet- ter taste.

With the introduction of the "American system," a new farce began. We no longer received our food in leaky wooden barrels. Instead, we formed a chow line and marched to the kitchen, one barrack at a time in a column of four, each column leading to the four windows from which the food was dispensed. Sometimes, it would occur that one window had a little thicker soup than the others, or that the fellow who dispensed it would scrape the bottom more often or had a dipper that wasn't dented, or he would pour it without spilling, or anything that appeared to offer more and better soup. And so, every noon hour, the men would ask those returning from the previous barrack questions like,

"Hey, Jack! How's the soup today" or "Which window, Joe?" or "Who's got the 'big' ladle today, Mike?" and, according to the answer they received, would fall into the proper lines.

The fourth window, having most of these attributes, it became the most popular line and was my favorite too. The cook at the window, a cheery-looking fellow named Mize, poured the soup carefully and scraped bottom, we thought, more often than the others. Another factor was that Hammond knew him when previously attached to M Company. As a result, we all lined up in back of Hammond. Hammonds would say a cheery "Hello, Mize" and we would all follow up by putting on a broad smile and making nice remarks like, "Soup looks good today, Mize," or "How goes it, Mize," or merely just laugh at what the one ahead of us said, so it would appear that we were all very pleasant people, all friends of Hammond's. It was a pure case of "ass kissing."

The soup wasn't the only part of the menu that improved. At about the same time, the bread situation improved too. Twice we were given an extra half ration (that made it four men to a loaf) and, occasionally thereafter, it was five men to a loaf instead of the usual six. This extra bread ration usually came on a Saturday and accompanied by cheese either soft sour pot cheese or a salted roll of hard cheese about two inches in diameter and less than an inch thick. On Sundays, meat was added to the usual bread ration. Often it was liverwurst, sometimes baloney or it was a mixture of three different kinds. The meat, however, never amounted to forty grams, which is about the meat you have on your little finger. On Mondays and Wednesdays and sometimes on Fridays, there was another innovation, marmalade, anywhere from forty to eighty grams at a time. What this marmalade was made of, we never knew. Hammond, our food expert, couldn't make up his mind whether it was made of apple jelly or a tomato mixture. It tasted good though, and it made the bread easier to digest. On Thursdays, our menu boasted of meat again but this was a practice they soon stopped. It was a can of chipped beef issued at twenty-four men to a can.

Everyone received a thimbleful, and we told them to throw it in the soup. I often thought they gave this merely to create confusion and dissension among the men, because the arguments weren't worth the meat we were getting. Some fellows argued for hours about the slightest difference between each other's ration.

And speaking of meat, we were all surprised one day while we were still being fed by the French, that one of the barrels contained an animal head (it has since been an oxen's, horse's, calf's, sheep's, etc.) complete with eyes and teeth. After much wrangling on who should nibble on this find, it was decided that the squad who brought it in should have the privilege. They got it, but I managed to get one of the teeth, a large molar which I still have—another souvenir. Too small for a horse, but too big for a sheep. I guess it came from a calf's head.

XII

"The Hungry and Sick"

The camp was running fairly smooth now. The food was still miserable but getting better; the guards didn't bother us, and we had already become accustomed to the lice. Gradually, a certain sense of security settled about the camp. The officers and non-coms had been moved to a new camp, and we had in charge a young private who seemed capable of talking with the Germans.

It was not unusual to see the Gestapo around. We knew it was the Gestapo because he wore civilian clothes, a long leather overcoat, thin-rimmed glasses, and carried a black bag, just like in the movies. An incident occurred at this time that brought a foreboding of future events. In mid-January, the Jewish boys were ordered segregated in another barrack. We protested that they were Americans, as we all were, but the Germans insisted that they be kept separate. Furthermore, they told us, any Jew who did not move and was caught would be severely dealt with. Many of the Jewish boys moved, since their names gave them away. Others hid their dog tags and decided to remain where they were and take their chances. At any rate, we were very pleased to learn, from the Jewish boys themselves, that they were allowed to visit with us at any time between 8:00 A.M. and 5:00 P.M., and that they were treated no worse than we were. The food they received was the same and the amount of coal (brickets) allotted to them was the same as ours. In fact, when it came, and the first Red Cross packages were distributed, they were the first to receive them. Thus, we got to believe that this segregation was just a formality. Jews were Jews to the German

High Command, but they were being treated as Americans despite the segregation. It was much like the Negro was treated in the South in our own country at that time.

Other than that incident, the camp was fairly quiet. But something was bound to go wrong. It was impossible for conditions to run smoothly for any length of time with 2,000 GIs lying around idly. There had to be some troublemakers in the crowd.

The serenity was broken on Sunday, January 28. We woke up that morning to find it already daylight. This was a surprise as "Caffe Hollen" usually got us out of bed at about the time that dawn was breaking, and as yet, he hadn't been around. In fact, the doors hadn't even been opened. For a while our minds were filled with wild expectations. "Maybe the Germans took off," somebody said. "Maybe Patton was already in Bad Orb." But one look out the window revealed to us that Patton was not in Bad Orb and that the Germans were still there, and with three times the force than we had ever seen before. Furthermore, they were all fully armed and wore German combat packs and helmets.

"They're probably just practicing," said Brummer. But the Germans were placing and loading their machines at all strategic positions and towers, by the fence, and even by the outside latrines. It all looked very ominous and like they meant business. Something was up.

It turned out to be their anger, for in a few moments, our guard unlocked the door and ordered us all outside. "And you'd better take your blanket and overcoat," somebody suggested. "You may be there for quite a while." This was not too encouraging. "Maybe it's another of those damn camp counts," someone remarked as we trudged outside.

They counted us all right, each barrack separately to make sure that nobody was missing and that there weren't any extra men in any one barrack. Then we were left to freeze for an hour in the snow, while Ernst, top barrack's leader for both sides of our barrack, went with the other barrack leaders to confer with Kasten, our confidence man for the entire American camp, and the Germans. At last he returned, but with the most frightening news since we got to the prison camp.

"Listen," he said, in his best English (he spoke with a slight German accent). "This is important. Last night, at about 7:00 o'clock, a German guard walked into the American kitchen for a last check. To his surprise, he found the door open. He switched on the lights and saw two feet sticking out from under the bread table. They apparently belonged to someone who was going to steal some food. Suddenly, he was attacked by someone else from behind, another GI, who struck him fourteen times on the head. Then, thinking he was dead, they ran away, and apparently made it back to their own barracks, though no one knows what barracks it is or how they got there.

"The Germans say there is blood all over the place and there are even chips from the guard's skull laying around. The guard, by some miracle, has not died yet, and he was able to tell the story before he fell into a coma. The men were definitely identified as GIs and not Russians with U.S. Army overcoats, for you guys that sold them.

"The Germans demand that these two men be found. There must be blood on their clothes because there was so much blood in the kitchen. They threaten to starve us until these men are found, no matter how long it takes. And if I know the Germans, they'll take hostages if they're not found."

If everyone's heart fell when they heard this, mine took a nose dive. I have probably never felt so low in my young life. A half-hour later, we were allowed to return to our barrack and locked in. Inside, all our clothes were inspected, but apparently the two malingerers were not from our barrack. There was nothing else to do now but wait for something to happen in the other barracks. Brummer and I went to bed. "That did it," I told Brummer for whatever the words meant. Brummer agreed. Charron and Durbin were sitting up in their bunks, Hammond and Yuskie were sitting in theirs. Turongian kept moving from one side of the barracks to the other, sniffing for rumors.

An hour later, Kasten entered our barrack and gave us a little speech as he had in all the other barracks. He asked that the man be turned over if they were from our barrack, as there was nothing else to do but starve if we didn't. He was followed by Father Patrick Hurley, the Catholic chaplain, one of the four officers who were allowed to remain in our camp. (The others were Chaplain O'Neill, a Protestant chaplain with whom D Company played football in England, a medic lieutenant, and a dental captain.) Father Hurley called the incident "a vicious act," since it was done in an attempt to cheat the next fellow out of his bread ration, and endangering, at the same time, the lives of two thousand men. There seemed to be no doubt in anyone's mind as to what the Germans might do if these two men were not produced.

Two more hours passed, during which time I managed to fall asleep for a few winks. When I awoke, rumors were flying again. Someone had heard that Ernst had been called out again. I was about to fall asleep once more when Ernst entered, and everyone began to yell, "At ease!"

"Listen," said Ernst after everyone had quieted down, "I have good news for you. We have caught the two men responsible for what happened last night, and they have admitted it." Brummer and I both leaped out of bed, and everyone was talking at once. "Listen!" cried Ernest, trying to raise his voice above the noise. "The Germans are so pleased that we turned them over so quickly that they're going to let us have the whole day's meal. The cooks are beginning to make the soup already. You'll get the soup at about four o'clock and the bread at about six-thirty along with the coffee."

The barrack cheered wildly. I could hardly believe it. For the first time, I managed to have some respect for our captors. They seemed satisfied just to get the men responsible for the acts. They could have just as well forgotten to feed us at all that day merely for punishment, or could have done many untold things, yet they were willing to give us not only the next meal, but the one we had missed at noon.

For the two men, it meant a German court-martial, and we all knew what that meant. Soon after, they were moved to another camp. Since then, I have heard that they were never killed and were eventually liberated. The guard himself, through some miraculous intercession, eventually recovered. Perhaps the fourteen or so strikes on the head and the chips on the floor was a gross exaggeration? It might have been. Nevertheless, it was a very foolish act committed by desperate men, who, knowing the Germans, had put the entire two thousand men in jeopardy.

The deathly whispers that were prevalent all morning was replaced by loud talk of happy people, and we played cards until sundown.

A few days later, we were ordered to clean our barracks extra good, to fix our bed as neatly as possible, and to try and look as presentable as we could. The camp commandant was coming around for an inspection. It didn't make much difference to us who was coming around, the commandant or Hitler himself. We had been forced to live in dirt, we might as well be in dirt during inspections. The German guard, however, advised us that it might be a good idea to make a good appearance before the commandant because, after all, he was the one who gave the orders, and if we could show him that we were still soldiers, able to make the best of the situation, and exercising common military courtesy, he might try to do his best for us in the way of getting more food or making things a bit more comfortable for us or giving us a break when it was possible. The commandant had already agreed not to feed us anymore greens because it caused much dysentery and diarrhea. We were now on a steady diet of pea, grits, or flour soup. Warren left it up to the men. We decided that, after all, we were still soldiers, American soldiers, and that the guard was probably right.

The commandant entered the barrack just before we were to line up for chow. This caused some grumbling because it meant waiting another half hour for our food, and since we were to be the last barrack to receive food that day, we were all quite hungry. When the commandant entered, some fool at the end of the barrack made a faux pas and yelled, *"Achtung!"* instead of "Attention!" We were all expecting the visit, and though we tried to be as sharp as possible, it took at least thirty seconds before everyone had jumped to the floor and was standing more or less at attention. The commandant, a major, walked through with a few of his aides, looked to his right and left, and finally stopped in the middle of the barrack, where he asked to see the barrack leader. As Ernst had gone to the office, Warren stepped forward. The commandant said something to him in German and then left. No sooner had the commandant left when Warren told us what he said.

"Now hold on to your shorts," he said, "we may be getting Red Cross packages tomorrow!"

A wild cheer followed, a cheer which the commandant must have surely heard outside.

Two days passed before we received our Red Cross package, and they seemed the longest two days we were to spend in the Stamlager. Negotiations for the packages had been going on for days. Some had arrived for us personally, and the Serbs were kind enough to let us have 500 packages of their own. We were to return them when our own arrived. As a result, we had to share one package among four men.

It is difficult for me to express the joy with which we received these packages, difficult for anyone who has never really been hungry to realize the satisfaction we were able to obtain from one quarter of an eleven-pound Red Cross package. Yet, that package meant more to us at the time, in that environment, than most anything in the world.

Turongian, Griffin, an acquaintance nearby and I were to share a package, and we decided to divide everything inside in four, regardless of how small or big it was. The first thing we divided were the cigarettes. Turongian just couldn't wait to get his hands on them. Smokers had been mixing weeds ever since they ran out of the real thing. The boys had long ago started trading with the Russians across the fence. Yuskie had already lost his shirt, at least he had sold it to the Russians for a few cigarettes and some cigarette paper. Hammond had sold his ring for fifteen cigarettes through Warren. Durbin did the same, and all had traded in their sweaters. Our package had Camels and Raleighs. There were five packages and we each received twenty-five cigarettes. Next we divided the tuna fish which we ate right there in the can. Then we shared the delicious peach ham and thirteen graham crackers. We cut the processed cheese next because I couldn't wait to sink my teeth into it, and the butter next, which was the biggest item in the package. Griffin wanted all his powdered milk at once so we shared that. We decided to keep the coffee in the can for anyone to use. There was some liverwurst, and we cut that up. Lastly, we divided the two chocolate bars, a box of raisins, and a box of sugar cubes, the latter amounting to twenty cubes each.

That night we ate like kings. I never saw so many different mixtures of food in my life. Some of us toasted our black bread and smeared it with butter and jam to make a delicious jelly roll. Others made a paste of their milk, mixed it with sugar and jam, threw in the raisins, and ate it like it was whipped cream and tutti frutti. Griffin didn't even bother to mix his milk with water; he ate most of it as it was. "Tastes damn good that way," he explained. I was inclined to agree with him, but I decided that I wanted my milk to last longer, so I mixed mine with water.

That night was one of the cheeriest we had at the Stamlager. The Germans let us borrow an accordion, and we sang loud and long, well past midnight. So loud, in fact, that surely the citizens of Bad Orb must have heard us. In a way, I believe it must have pleased most of the Germans to see us happy if only because the happier we were, the less trouble they would have with us. But then, that seemed to be the German strategy in the prison camps. First, they would starve you to near death, making you as miserable as possible until they finally decided to give you a little extra, which would make you think they were angels. Of course, there are those who will say that the Germans had little food even for themselves. But ask the boys who were captured in 1943, when the Germans still occupied most of Europe, what they were fed. They would give you the same menu of erzatz coffee, black bread and soup. The only thing that kept them alive until liberation in 1945 was the Red Cross packages that they received at regular intervals until January 1945, when Red Cross deliveries broke down and the men were forced to march hundreds of miles from east to west and vice versa ahead of the liberating armies, when they were lucky to get even bread. We were told that what we were fed was the same that the German citizen was getting in Bad Orb. Yet I never saw anyone in Germany that had withered and melted away into a mass of bones such as we had.

I sang myself hoarse that night. By the time I got to bed, I had eaten everything but a piece of cheese, most of the butter, some milk, coffee, and half the raisins. About the cigarettes, Charron and I had a little talk concerning what we should do with them, since we were the only two nonsmokers in the bunch. In England, Charron's cigarette ration would go to Durbin and mine would go to Walker. Charron had no sooner received his Red Cross ration when Durbin took them, assuming that Charron would give him the whole ration.

But times were different. I told Charron, and they had no right to expect the entire ration, nor any at all for that matter, even if we were to give it to them. "I don't care what they think," I told him, "I'm only giving them half my ration. They'll probably smoke most of them, but they'll be trading some of it for bread also. And why shouldn't we be able to trade some too. Remember when Yuskie had cigarettes when we first got here. He ate, and I didn't see him offer anybody any of the extra food he was getting. The boys were lucky to get a few puffs from the cigarettes he was smoking."

Charron agreed with me. He had not intended to give them all his cigarettes, but since Durbin had taken them, he hesitated to ask for them. He was waiting to see what I would do, and after I told him, he asked Durbin for his cigarettes. Durbin returned them, but he was so offended that he wouldn't accept the half-ration that Charron offered him. But Hammond was practical. He took the half-ration, which he put into a pool for the boys. I gave mine to Turongian with the same understanding.

I often wondered whether I would regret this move. I wondered whether I had been selfish in not offering all my cigarettes. After all, we were all buddies, it seemed. I could tell that they were very angry with us, especially Durbin, who never forgave Charron. I saw, then, that we weren't going to be too happy living together from then on, especially when the cigarettes ran out. Then the battle would begin again, the five smokers, namely Durbin, Hammond, Turongian, Brummer, and Yuskie, against the two nonsmokers Charron and me.

Everything went well for a few days. I finished the last of my raisins, one by one the next day. The lumps of sugar, I ate likewise because they tasted so good. The cheese, I finished during the night and was already buying more at the exhorbitant price of two cigarettes for half a ration. The coffee, I mixed with the morning brew, though I confess, it didn't improve the taste any; as a matter of fact, it tasted worse! The last thing I finished was the milk, and that went the following afternoon. The only thing I had left were three cigarettes, which I was determined to hold for another week when they would be scarce again and the bartering brisker.

Charron, meanwhile, had met with some bad luck. The very night the Red Cross package was distributed, he fell sick, and the next day when he woke up, he was yellow as a chicken. I knew immediately that it was yellow jaundice, because I had it once myself when I was twelve years old. What had brought this about was pretty obvious, and since we came to the camp, several cases of yellow jaundice had occurred. Jaundice is an illness of the liver in which the intestines leading to the liver close up because of lack of nourishment. As a result, the slightest bit of food is filling, and poor Charron was unable to receive any enjoyment from most of his Red Cross package. Eventually, he gave everything away, much of it to his bunk partner Durbin. Durbin offered him his milk since he claimed he disliked milk in any form.

Charron was unable to eat not only his part of the Red Cross package but also his usual meals. At noon, he would eat only half his soup, the rest he would usually give to Durbin. At night, he would eat a small chunk of bread and share the rest of it with the boys. It made us feel a little awkward. Every night we would sit on the upper bunks and as usual talk about food and home. And then there would be a long silence, during which we were all self-conscious of waiting for Charron to share with us the bread he had placed in his box. When Charron finally told Durbin to divide the bread among the boys, we all felt a little embarrassed. However, that did not stop us from accepting the piece. Hunger has no pride. After we had eaten the small chunk, we talked for a few moments and then went to bed with a "Thanks, Charron" or "Thank you, Charron" or "Thanks a lot, Charron. Hope you feel better in the morning."

XIII

Hangin' In

The afternoon of February 5th was one of the saddest we were to spend at the Stamlager. For a few days now, rumor had it that the Jewish boys were to be moved to a new camp. This, we were told, was for the purpose of getting a new American camp readied for us near Leipzig. With them was to go Kasten, our American "confidence" man. Another fellow whom we knew only as Eddy was to take his place. This sounded like a harmless story the Germans gave us, but there was one peculiarity that made most of us suspicious of the whole idea. To go along with the Jews, a number of men were chosen from each barrack.

These men, we understood, were the "undesirables" of the camp, people who had caused some trouble at one time or another and made things uncomfortable at the camp. Why were the "undesirables" being sent out with the Jews? If we were going to end up at the same place, what difference did it make who went first? Obviously, the Germans were merely cleaning up the camp of those people who caused them the most trouble, either ideologically or actually. We began to suspect that the Germans never intended for them to open a new camp or for us to follow.

In choosing the men who became the "undesirables," Ernst, in order that he might shirk the full responsibility of naming the men, suggested that if anyone had any complaints against anyone or had seen anyone steal from his buddy, he should register it with him, and the information would be kept in the strictest confidence. Whether anyone did, I don't know, though I believe some did. At any rate, most of the troublemakers were chosen to ship out, while a few, who might have exercised some influence with Ernst, remained.

Most of the men realized, as we did, that both the Jews and the "undesirables" were being shanghied out of camp. Rosenburg knew it too when he came to say good-bye that afternoon. He gave each of us his address, and we gave him ours. Then he insisted that we give him any photograph that we might have of ourselves. We were the best bunch of buddies that he ever knew, he told us. He said that he wanted to remember us all when we got home and that he would write us. And as he shook hands with each of us, he burst out in a flood of tears. We were all visibly moved by Rosey's farewell, and if we didn't cry too, it was because we may not have been the greatest bunch of guys he thought we were, or maybe we weren't in his shoes. I can tell you, though, that each of us had a big lump in our throats when Rosey left. Charron and I gave him what remained of our cigarettes, and Hammond gave Rosey some of the cigarettes they had pooled together.

Zeke Zimand came in to say good-bye. If Zimand was worried about moving out, he didn't show it. He had always been a don't-give-a-damn, happy-go-lucky character from Brooklyn. Short, squat, a dark heavy growth that would cover his face even when he had just shaved. His eyes squinted as a smile would suddenly come over his round face, and you couldn't help but smile with him. I met him at Camp Upton, from where we left together for ASTP training at Fort Benning, Georgia. They put us in charge of fifteen men on the train, and he nearly caused a riot. At Benning, he was always on the "TS" list. When we got to Atterbury, regardless of how much he was hated by the sergeant, they just couldn't help but laugh at his nonchalant attitude or his lazy shuffle around the company area. I said so-long to Zeke and was sorry to see him go.

B. J. Vogel came to say good-bye too, as did Norman Martin.

"I'll drop you a line when we get back to New York," I told BJ, who lived in Brooklyn. I didn't know it, but BJ would never get to see Brooklyn again.

Some of the story of what happened to the boys on the way to Leipzig was told to me a few months after I returned to the States by Norman Martin whom I met at the Polo Grounds on Eisenhower Day. I didn't ask him too much because he himself had to move about with a cane, was still suffering from yellow jaundice, and had several front teeth missing. I didn't think he wanted to talk too much about it. He told me that of all the men who left, at least one hundred did not return, among them B.J. Vogel. Ouimet, our bugler, and ex-sergeant Rowe, both of whom were not Jews or "undesirables" but merely included because they were extras in one of the barracks, died also, Rowe having been beaten to death. I felt sorry for Rowe. He had been married ten years and was the father of three nice kids. Somehow, it struck me that his fate had been decided long before his death, on that very day in England when he was stripped of his rank. Had he not lost his stripes he would have been transferred to Ziegenheim along with the rest of the noncoms, and in all probability, would be with his kids now.

I asked about Rosenburg and Zimand. Zimand, he said, was okay. As for Rosenburg, he didn't know how he ever made it, but he did, though the last he had heard of him, he was in the hospital, quite sick. I felt sorry for BJ, Ouimet, and Rowe, and it made me mad to think that they should have died so unnecessarily. Kasten, the ill-fated camp "confidence" man who had been shipped out mostly because he was getting too shrewd with the Germans, barely escaped death himself. The day before his liberation, he was caught with sticks of dynamite in his pockets and had been ordered shot. The Germans, however, never got around to it.

The days moved slowly. At about the same time that Charron was recovering from his jaundice, I became sick myself, though it didn't disturb my appetite any. What I was suffering from most was a bad cold which I couldn't get rid of, and which had plugged up my ears so much that I couldn't hear a person talking to me three feet away. Because of this, I became the subject of many jokes and much ridicule, which really didn't bother me one way or the other because I couldn't hear them anyway.

By this time, the boys had run out of cigarettes. As a result, they were tense and nervous. And when they got tense, there came a period when they had to explode before they become normal again. Naturally, they had to have someone to explode at; in this case who were the most obvious ones but Charron and me. They hated Charron especially. He had just sold his school ring for some cigarettes, which made them jealous since they had sold just about everything they owned. They also disliked the idea of giving him a ration of jam between the five of them for one of his cigarettes. They felt that as a buddy, Charron should give it to them, but they never explained why they didn't do the same when they had cigarettes.

Charron, however, didn't see any consolation in selling his school ring just so the boys could smoke. He gave them a few cigarettes, but he intended to trade the rest for food. When Charron did trade with the boys for jam, it was because he wanted to see the boys smoke. Actually, he didn't care for the jam; he could have received a third of a ration of bread for the same cigarette. The boys offered him a third of a ration of bread once, but Charron wouldn't accept it because he didn't want it to seem like he was taking bread out of their mouths. Turongian convinced him that he might as well have it as anyone else, since they were going to trade it with someone else anyway. When Charron finally agreed and the boys had smoked their cigarette, Brummer grunted, "I'll never trade any of *my* bread off again."

Charron hated to even eat with them. He told me once, "If I'm eating a little more, they think I'm a louse. If I try to eat somewhere else, they start cursing me." When he finally realized that he couldn't satisfy them no matter what he did, he decided not to barter with them at all. This made them hate him even more, because it cost them two rations of jam to get a cigarette somewhere else.

They hated me because I agreed with Charron. I thought they were being selfish, and I told them so.

"It looks like you fellows forgot about the bread and the soup he passed around when he couldn't eat," I said looking directly at Durbin.

"We gave him our jam," said Turongian, "so he could swallow what he could eat better, didn't we? Durbin gave him his milk. What was he going to do with the bread anyway, let it grow stale and throw it out?"

"If he was somebody else," I said, "he could have sold it for cigarettes or money, which he could have used later when he got hungry again."

"Maybe you'd do that," said Hammond.

"No, I wouldn't, and neither would Charron," I retorted. "That's why he gave it to you. And he gave you half the ration of cigarettes, didn't he?"

At this point, Durbin burst forth with a diatribe so vicious that it convinced me that he was behind the whole hate-Charron attack.

"Who do you think bought all the candy for him on the boat," he cried. "He didn't have a damn cent. I spent a lot of money on him—"

"I suppose," I said, "that he should be indebted to you for the rest of his life." Then I brought up the cigarettes Charron had given him in England.

The arguing, of course, got us nowhere. Nobody can reason well on an empty stomach. As for me, they disliked me so much more.

Their dislike toward my writing, I mentioned before. They felt that I didn't spend enough time with them, that I didn't play enough cards with them, that I didn't drool enough about food with them. On that count, I can see some justification for their jealousy. Perhaps I wasn't as good a companion much of the time as I might have been. It wasn't that I disliked their company in any way. I was very glad to find myself in the same barrack with them, just as glad to sleep in the same corner with them. Certainly during my stay at the Stamlager, I did not seek any other companions. Yet I could not see myself sitting on the top bunk with them playing hearts and rummy day in and day out, talking about nothing but candy and food, driving myself crazy with the very thought of it, listening to the silly, petty squabbles that arose every time someone said something that was interpreted another way by someone else.

Actually, I played a great deal of cards with them during the day. I should have liked a dollar for every game of hearts that I played. It would give me a sizeable sum, though the others would have been set for life. After supper when the shutters were closed, it was impossible to write because of the meager light in the barrack; there was nothing else to do but talk, and the talk always managed to get around to food, regardless of what we began with. Could I be blamed for wanting to pass my time doing something that took my mind off the things that were making me miserable?

In another sense, I began to dislike sitting up with the boys ever since my ears had gone bad. Quite often they would make me look pretty ridiculous. Everything they said to me had to be repeated. For that reason I disliked to talk about anything. Sometimes, they purposely made it more difficult for me to understand them. Brummer, for instance, who usually spoke so fast that I had difficulty knowing what he said even when my ears were well, began to speak even faster, and often softer, so that I couldn't make heads or tails of what he was saying, regardless of what he said. Often, too, he would make up words of his own while I was trying to figure out what he was talking about. The others would laugh and giggle. I could see that the boys were having a good time in this way. In a sense, it amused me. It reminded me of a funny movie I had once seen. I pretended not to care, for the sake of avoiding stupid arguments which would probably make me look silly.

"Raf," Charron said to me one day, "you should hear what they're saying about you! They call you every name you can think of right in front of you, just because you can't hear."

"Well," I said, pretending not to be hurt, "at least we can't say they're talking behind my back, can we? Let the boys have their fun, so long as it makes them happy. I'll tell you this much, though, right now, the boys are one big happy family together. But the day is going to come when they're going to get tired of arguing with us and they're going to argue with each other. And it won't be long either. Brummer and Durbin have already started it, and the day Durbin breaks up with Hammond, then the real fun begins."

Charron laughed at the thought of it. Then he mused seriously.

"I can't understand Durbin," he said. "We used to be such good buddies."

"Yes," I agreed and the words reminded me of Bob Walker. "You know," I told Charron, "I hope Bob is okay. Up until now I was hoping that, assuming he got captured, he was with us. But now I'm glad he's not. I'd hate to think that he might be on their side."

The days dragged on. During those days, the one thing that we kept looking for besides food were the daily news reports we received at noon every day. Soon after we arrived at the Stamlager, the Germans had permitted us to receive news reports on the progress of the war. The information, of course, was German edited and delivered over a radio broadcast called "Wehrmach Sprecht," which our "confidence" man was permitted to listen to. He, in turn, relayed it to the barracks leaders, and we received it from them.

Sometimes the "Wehrmach Sprecht" spoke the truth. They were especially truthful about their losses on the Eastern front. The Russians were overrunning their land at the rate of twenty miles a day, and the Germans did not hesitate to admit it, sometimes, even exaggerating their plight. There were other times, however, when they were ridiculously cautious about their news. After the Russians had taken Budapest, the Germans insisted that they were still holding a castle in the southern suburb of the city. They dramatized this castle in every news report for at least three weeks until they came around to admitting that the Russians were a good fifty miles past Budapest at that time.

About the Western front, the Germans were very cautious about giving out their own news. They seemed to stress most of what was important on the Russian side. When we first learned that the Americans had reached the Rhine and the British were trying to break through the plains of Hanover, the Germans put a complete blackout on the news of that front for at least ten days. Meanwhile, I made myself a little map, which I copied from a neighbor's address book, and began shading in the area already occupied by the Allies. Each day, there would be a little more to shade.

With all the wonderful news we were getting, speculation began immediately as to the actual date of liberation. Some predicted it would be as early as February 15th, but the 15th passed without even a rumble, and they chose March 1st. Others, like Hammond, said it would be March 15th, and Yuskie decided that if it wasn't by then, he would make a break for it. Others decided it would be around April 1st, Easter Sunday. One fellow, a scrawny little pessimist, was less optimistic.

"Ahhh, you guys are nuts," he exclaimed. "You'll be lucky to get out by the 4th of July."

"Shaddup" was the uncomplimentary epithets. Brummer and I were hoping to be home by Mother's Day.

It was a beautiful, crystal-clear February afternoon, and we had just had our soup. Some of us were preparing to play cards on Charron's bunk, when we heard the drone of an airplane approach in the distance. Someone put his head to the window and looked up. There were two planes approaching, both heading straight for our barrack! Within moments, they were upon us when one dived and the second followed right behind. Suddenly there was a burst of gunfire overhead! Immediately there was panic in the barrack as most of us dropped to the floor and scattered under beds. Bullets zoomed overhead and swept back up in the air, seemingly in perfect formation as the second followed the first. Luckily, they didn't come back.

This was the most nerve-wracking experience we were to have at the Stamlager. Apparently, a British fighter was having a dog-fight with a German fighter. The German plane, realizing that there was a camp nearby, and getting the worst of it, decided to fly over the camp, which was identified by a big POW on the roof, in the hope that the British plane would not fire at him there. The British fighter apparently didn't see it, or recognize it, and fired away. The whole episode lasted about a minute with the burst about ten seconds. When it was over, everyone slowly emerged from hiding places, but still scared to death. One fellow, who happened to be in the washroom at the time, emerged as white as a sheet with a shredded hole in his jacket, and unable to speak. A bullet had passed right by him and it came so close to his anatomy that had he been the normal weight instead of what he had already lost at the Stamlager, it would have ripped his stomach open.

Most of the damage was recorded by Serbs in the barrack in back of us. Three men were killed, and some others were hurt. From that day on, we decided that, if anything, the outside latrines provided some protection from this kind of invasion. The next day, several of us were digging in the outside latrines. But the enthusiasm died out in a couple of days, and the shovels were put to rest. The Serbs, on the other hand, kept digging until well into the day we got liberated, and we watched as the shovels slowly disappeared from view as the latrines got deeper.

The days moved along, each day the same as the other. Monday seemed like Tuesday, Tuesday like Friday, Friday like Wednesday, etcetera. Sometimes you might lose track of the date, but it didn't make much difference anyway. Only Sunday seemed firm in the Stamlager.

When Sunday rolled around, some of us would go to church. For our barrack Sunday Mass for the Protestants was in the morning, while for the Catholics it was in the afternoon. Brummer and Durbin would go in the morning, and Charron and I in the afternoon. We didn't always go; in fact, there were more times that we didn't than we did. Usually though, when we didn't go on Sunday, we would try to "made up for it" during the week.

Many words have been used to describe the work of the Army chaplains both behind the lines and at the front. Yet to me, I shall always remember the work of two men. Chaplains Hurly and Neal, who stayed behind to watch over the souls and morals (as well as morale) of two thousand battered, wasting individuals, and to bring them some comfort and peace through the words of God at a time they needed it most. I like to think that these people saved more lives than even the doctors could have, had the doctors received an abundance of German medicinal supplies.

Chaplain Neal, the Protestant chaplain, was known to us from Atterbury. He was a very active individual, a good preacher and story teller, and a fine athlete. Quite often, on Saturday afternoons, he would join the boys in a game of football. D Company must have been his favorite, for I saw him several times dashing around the battalion area with our boys. After we arrived at the Stamlager, he had his choice of remaining with the men or being shipped out and perhaps repatriated back to the Allies, since there was supposed to be an exchange of chaplains between the combatants. He, of course, chose to remain.

He gathered the Protestant boys together, held prayer meetings every day, and services every Sunday. He also formed a fine choral group with some of the men whose voices were better than average. Every morning he found the energy to run around the camp at least once, which was something that no one else did. At one time, he caught the mumps, and for a time we were worried about him. He recovered, however, though he did miss his exercise for about a week. Of course, he was eating a bit more than we were at the time. He received an extra liter of soup each day, a privilege extended only to chaplains, doctors, first-aid men, and barrack's leaders. Not that the Germans were giving any more; the cooks merely added that much more water.

Father Hurley, the Catholic chaplain, was a less active man, physically, and a little older. I believe he was a member of the 28th Division; at least we had never seen him with the 106th, though I heard it mentioned once that he may have been attached to division headquarters. Father Hurley also chose to stay behind to take care of the spiritual needs of the Catholic boys. He held mass every morning in Barrack 42B. (It was empty and also served as our "recreational" room in the afternoon.)

Since the Catholic Mass required some additional items, which he didn't have, Father Hurley asked the Germans for permission to travel twenty miles to a nearby Italian prisoner of war camp, where he was able to obtain some bare essentials. He managed to get a supply of hosts for Holy Communion that would last about four months, some wine, and the proper vestments.

As he could not obtain a printed copy of the Latin prayers that were read as part of the Mass, he was forced to copy them word for word on paper, and later recopy them in ink. At one time, someone spilled water on them, blurring the writing, which made it more difficult for him. It was unfortunate, too, that one day someone stole Father Hurley's Communion host, thinking, possibly, that it was the kind of bread he might fill his stomach on. Father Hurley requested that the host be returned, and in such a manner where he would not have to know who the thief was. The host was returned.

At Mass, Father Hurley always preached for about ten minutes, and what he said often cheered us up. He had a wonderful speaking voice and an excellent manner of expressing himself. His powerful words always gave us the feeling of confidence and reassurance.

Father Hurley formed a Holy Name Society, which received Holy Communion every week. Upon liberation, he requested every Catholic in camp to turn his name in. At Christmas time that year, we all received a membership card which read: "This is to certify that (name) is a charter member of the Holy Name Society of Our Lady of Mt. Carmel Parish, Stamlager IX B, Bad Orb, Germany." It was signed, Father E. J. Hurley, Pastor.

I have already mentioned our "recreation" room. Actually, there wasn't much offered there in the way of recreation. At one time, the Germans permitted one of our men to travel to a British hospital, about fifteen miles away, where he was given a number of books and several games which they had received from the British Red Cross. Thus, a small, lending library and a game room was formed in the aforementioned Barrack 42B for anyone who wished to idle away a few hours. The books themselves were mostly mysteries with some classics available, and the games ranged from simple Parcheesi and Polly Anna to a British Monopoly. For most of the men who would take advantage of the limited facilities, it meant a means of passing the few hours between meals.

Day by day the news kept getting better and better until, finally, it was getting so good on the Western front that the Germans put a news blackout on it for several days. We realized that with the Americans poised on one side of the Rhine, it would not be long before they could be on the other side, and with our camp just sixty miles from Mainz and thirty-five miles from Frankfort, liberation was not too far away; that is, if they didn't pull us out of there beforehand.

Finally, after nine days of rumors, during which time we kept hearing the rumble of bombs and artillery in the distance, we learned, through the "Wehrmacht Sprecht" that the Americans had established a bridgehead at Ramegan. When it was learned that the bridgehead had been widened the next day, we knew that it was only a matter of time. At the same time, we learned that the Russians were making headway in the East, too. This was evidenced by the fact that we were ordered to move from our current barrack, 44, to another barrack, 31. This was necessary, they told us, because a thousand captured British troops were coming to our camp. They had been camped in Poland and Upper Silesia when the Germans had to move them cross-country because the Russians were getting too close. They had been walking for thirty-one days and traveled nearly 800 miles, during which time they had lost several men because of pneumonia and lack of nourishment.

No sooner had we moved into Barrack 31 when a thousand more men came in from Limberg to the north. They had been marching about ten days as the Americans were moving in. Many of the men were from the 106th Division. I met one of my friends from ASTP who had been placed in a different company at Atterbury along with several other pals of mine. I asked him whether he had seen any of them. He told me that the last time he had seen them was during the Bulge, but they became separated when they left Limberg and he remained. I asked him how the food was in Limberg.

"Same stuff you're getting here," he told me, "except that at Limberg, we were getting rations every night from Argentine Red Cross packages. Once in a while we'd get a chocolate bar, or some cheese, or sometimes a cigarette."

At about this time, we received our second Red Cross package. It had been well over a month since we received our first, and we were beginning to think that we were never going to get another. This time, we expected an entire package apiece since we had been told that the Red Cross was to send enough to last us for quite a while. But when the packages arrived, we were told that during the trip, the train had been bombed and machine gunned with the result that many of the packages had been burned or destroyed. From what remained, we owed the Serbs five hundred packages, we had to give the British some, and all that remained for us was a third of a package apiece. This was quite a disappointment, but we were satisfied to get that.

This time, in order to avoid further arguments with anybody, Charron and I decided that we wouldn't give the boys any cigarettes at all. This would really make them fume, we thought, but they had their own rations to keep them for a while.

The minute we got the package, the boys were happy again. We were all one big happy family. Hammond was the first to express his friendliness towards us.

"From now on, boys," he said, "no more arguing. Shake!" We shook.

Hammond, I believe, suspected all the while that they weren't going to receive any cigarettes and I believe, that he meant it in all sincerity at the time. People have a tendency to forget their differences on a full stomach. Even Durbin managed to say a few words to Charron. But even if what was said was said in all sincerity, we knew that their attitude would change the minute they were out of cigarettes. However, if their remarks were meant to play on our sympathies, they didn't succeed. Charron and I pooled our cigarettes and kept them for ourselves.

Personally, I had wanted to give Turongian some cigarettes for himself. I had always liked Turongian, and I felt sorry for him. So did Charron. But if we had given Turongian some, he would have shared them with the rest of the boys, which of course was perfectly natural and correct. But to us, it meant merely contributing to their pool, which we did not intend to do. Had we given Turongian the cigarettes with the understanding that he smoke them himself, he had a perfect right to feel unfriendly towards us because we would be asking him not to share with his friends after they had shared theirs with him. And had he taken them and smoked them himself, his friends would have turned on him for the same reason. For the sake of avoiding arguments with everyone involved, we decided to make no exception.

Meanwhile, my prophesy about the boys was, sadly, becoming true. Not only did they find it hard to be friends with us, they could hardly be friends with each other. When the boys received their second Red Cross package, Yuskie decided that he wasn't going to pool his with the boys. During our stay at camp, Yuskie must have been the hungriest man in the camp. He was so hungry sometimes that in order that the hours between the meals go faster, he buried his head under the covers and went to sleep. Now Yuski decided he wanted to go on his own and buy some food for himself with some of his cigarettes. The boys didn't like this, because Yuskie was not one to control himself very well and, in all probability, he would have run out of cigarettes before they did, and they knew what that meant.

"Okay," said Hammond, "but when you finish them, don't be coming back to us."

"Don't worry," mumbled Yuskie.

Yuskie of course ran out of his before the boys did, and though he didn't ask the boys for a puff, you could tell that he was dying for one. Eventually, they allowed him a puff or two, now and then.

Brummer, meanwhile got himself into an occasional argument with Hammond. I can't say what they argued about. Usually it was over a trivial matter that was never worth the energy they spent over it. In fact, sometimes it was so stupid that it usually ended like this:

"Yeah?"

"Yeah!"

"Oh, Brummer, you're so dumb and stubborn sometimes!"

"You think you're so smart, huh? You think you're so smart!"

"Yeah!"

"Yeah?"

"I don't want to argue with you anymore."

"What's the matter? Maybe you ain't so smart, huh?"

"Oh, shut up! You can't argue."

"Oh, you can?"

"Yeah!"

"Yeah!"

Sometime later, Durbin would get into an argument with Brummer. It would usually end up the same except that Durbin, true to form of all hot-heads, would usually walk away in a blaze of fury, with his hands in his pockets.

Then Hammond would interject.

"I don't know what's wrong with Durbin. He's all nerves."

Turongian, when he chose to argue, argued against anybody as long as he thought he was right. Usually, his arguments were more sensible than the rest, if that really can be said of men who are desperate to hang onto their sanity. I often thought he took too much at times. Once, at the end of one argument, Hammond called him a dirty dog because of his actions back at the Schnee Eiffel. Turongian didn't say a word but gave him his dirtiest look. I could tell that he was hurt, though, and I think Hammond sensed it too, because he never called him that again, at least not to his face.

When they found it tiresome to argue among themselves, and when they came to realize that we weren't paying much attention to them when they were arguing with us, they decided to argue with Griffin, who was now sleeping directly across the barrack in 31.

Brummer hated Griffin. Griffin was a member of the original cadre that helped form the 106th Division. Brummer joined the outfit at its inauguration, and Griffin, he said, was a first-class louse all through basic training. Now, he was taking it out on him by razzing him about the stripes he lost and how it served him right. But Brummer only spoke like that when Hammond was having it out with Griffin. Otherwise, you could see the two of them alone sometimes, talking about old times in South Carolina and about maneuvers in Tennessee.

Hammond, who joined D Company the day we left Atterbury after he had been thrown out of M Company, had always hated Griffin. Griffin one day told him to do something, and Hammond asked why?

"Because I told you to," sneered Griffin, and Hammond never forgot it. When Griffin was demoted, Hammond spent most of his time teasing Griffin about the good time they were going to have on KP together.

One day, while we were still in Barrack 31, Warren wanted the names of those men who needed blankets to sleep under. Griffin asked me to turn his name in. Immediately, Brummer and Hammond both jumped on him. "What's the matter, Griffin, you want special privileges?" What's the matter, Griffin—"

"Look," I finally told them, "mind your own business and leave the guy alone, will you? He asked me; he didn't ask you."

"What are you sucking ass for?" Hammond responded. "He's no sergeant anymore. He can't do nothing to you anymore. He can't hurt you anymore."

I figured I might as well not bother to answer him, since I could have gotten more satisfaction out of banging my head against the wall.

"Don't pay any attention to them," I told Griffin later. "You know how it is, nerves. They haven't been smoking lately."

"I know," said Griffin. "But you know, Raf, I wouldn't have thought of it from at least four of them."

While we were still in Barrack 45, Hammond struck up an argument with someone two beds away. This was about the price and weight of hogs and how they were to be cut after they were slaughtered. We heard this one for days.

During all these arguments, Yuskie had very little to say. He was too hungry.

While the cigarettes lasted, the boys were happy. Besides getting their few puffs regularly, they had cigarettes to spare and with which they bought bread and potatoes in the black market. Charron and I were doing the same. In the beginning, we were in the market for milk. We bought Durbin's because he insisted he didn't like it. Later, we bought bread and potatoes not only because we realized we needed more solids, but because we had to be careful of the milk vendors.

Some people, it seems, haven't got a heart, much less a brain. When they're up against it, they will do anything just to satisfy their own stomachs. It justifies my theory that it takes a GI to screw another GI. One fellow came in one day boasting of the wonderful buy he made, a whole can of powdered milk for just twenty-four cigarettes. Not bad, thought Charron and I, but we changed our minds a few minutes later when the "lucky" customer found that he hadn't bought a whole can of milk after all, but three-quarters of a can full of old rags. The shrewd profiteer had covered the rags with just about enough milk to make it look good. The customer had even tested it with a stick before he bought it and when the stick hit bottom he was convinced he had a can of milk. But he got stuck with it.

Another shrewd merchant pulled another stunt. Instead of filling most of the can with rags, he filled it with something that looked more like the milk that he was selling, the white lime that was being used in our latrines. Luckly, the person who bought it realized before he drank it. They went looking for this would-be murderer later, but they could never associate anyone with the can.

Soon, however, we were all out of cigarettes and so were the boys. Charron, however, still had a thousand francs in his pocket, which he had managed to hold onto.

"Look!" he told me one day, "this money isn't doing me any good. I was saving to buy my wife something in case we hit Paris or the Riviera after we're liberated. But if we do get there, we'll get some kind of pay there anyway, so I might as well put this to some good use. I'll see if I can get a loaf of bread for it, and we'll share it."

I told him that it was very generous of him to want to share it with me, but that if he didn't I wouldn't feel hurt or offended, because, after all, it was his money and I didn't have any money to give him. But he insisted that we share. I promised that I would pay him back, at least half the money, when we got back to the States. Though I'm ashamed to admit it, I have yet to keep my promise.

Charron looked up a BTO (Big Time Operator) we called "Frenchy," and asked him if he could get a loaf of bread for a thousand francs. Frenchy thought he might swing it. The next day, he came around with a nice big loaf of German black bread. When we sat down to eat it, Charron and I looked at each other. He cut off a good-sized heel and gave it to the boys. Then he cut the rest of it up into slices, and Charron and I ate it.

I often wondered what they were thinking of as they ate their bread. I'm sure that they weren't thinking too kindly of me. I could almost read what was going on in their minds. "We get the heel for five men," they were saying, "while Raffa gets to eat a third of the loaf."

A few days later, we got another Red Cross package. Again we expected at least one package for two men but the cart that was taking them from Bad Orb up to our camp was machine gunned, with the result that we received only one package for eleven men.

On Holy Thursday, we got two surprises: we got our second delousing in the morning and another Red Cross package in the evening. The second delousing, coming exactly three months from our first one, was welcome, but hardly relevant, as we itched the minute we got back into the same lousy clothes. The Red Cross package was hardly relevant either as we were to share it twenty-one men to a package. There was more cheese on the makeshift knife than what went down our throats.

By now the situation was getting bad as far as the food was concerned. We were getting less bread at night and our soup began to get more watery. However, the guns were getting closer each time, and on Holy Thursday night, we could see flares going up in the not-too-far-distance and the shells coming close enough to shake the barrack. "Any day now," we kept telling each other. "Any day now, if they don't decide to move us out," I muttered trying to be less optimistic than I really was to hope.

On Good Friday, we learned that the Germans were trying to move the prisoners out of the camp. They started with the Serbs (their latrine digging was interrupted), but after leaving that morning, they returned that night. The Germans concluded it was too late to move anyone out. The Americans had already surrounded the camp for a ten-mile radius. This brought cheers from everyone in the camp.

On Saturday, the artillery sounded so close that we knew it would be only a matter of time, perhaps twenty-four hours. By then, there were only about ten guards left in the camp; the others had either been sent away or had taken off. The guards that were left didn't even bother to lock the doors at night anymore, and those who stood at the high turrets that surrounded the camp had removed their machine guns and merely stood on the ground so that any Americans who might come up the road would not take any pop shots at them. That night, we assigned a number of men to stand by each barrack to prevent anyone who tried to break out of the camp.

On Easter Sunday, April 1, Charron and I attended Mass. We could hear American machine guns rattling away in what seemed to be just outside Bad Orb. I shall never forget that day, and I scratched the following on a piece of a piece of paper after Mass:

Today, besides being April Fool's Day, was also Easter Sunday. Easter Services in the form of a High Mass were held in the Recreation Hall at the unusual hour of 9:15 A.M.

Mass today was somehow much more beautiful than it had ever been before at the Stamlager, and it will probably never be more beautiful or more appreciated than it was today, anywhere. The Kyrie and the other solemn passages of the Mass were all beautifully sung by the choir, and at the end of the mass, we all sung an original song written for the occasion.

What impressed me most was Father Hurley's sermon on this Easter Sunday. No one probably delivered a more appropriate sermon at a more appropriate time.

"I would have liked to announce this Easter," he began, "that we were now liberated. Now it seems that they are having just a little trouble getting here, close as they are, so we'll have to wait it out for a few hours more.

"Easter Sunday, to us especially, should have a special meaning. Though for all practical purposes, we are liberated, we were here, prisoners and oppressed, and for a little over three months, we sweated out our liberation. Yet look at the world. They were prisoners even when Adam created the first sin against God, until Easter Sunday when Christ rose from the dead and ascended into heaven. And when Christ died and rose from the dead, Easter Sunday, was liberation for the world. And so, Easter Sunday was liberation for us, too. We should be doubly thankful."

And Easter Sunday *was* our liberation. At 7:35 P.M., after we had been locked in by the German guards, it was announced that the camp had been officially turned over to the Americans. We had been liberated.

I could have added something else to Father Hurley's sermon, something which made it more glorious. We had arrived at Bad Orb on Christmas Day, when Christ came into the world to liberate it from sin and oppression, and we were liberated on Easter Sunday, the day Christ rose from the dead.

XIV

Deliverance

It was 6:30 A.M. the next morning that we saw the first American troops arrive at our camp. They were the Second Reconnaisance outfit of the 7th Division, who arrived in jeeps, tanks, and half-tracks. The manner in which they were greeted was something not to be forgotten. We swarmed the vehicles like locusts, steal-ing every can and box of American rations we could lay our hands on. Some greedy characters weren't satisfied with stealing food; they also stole anything that they could lay their hands on, especially pistols and knives that the reconnaisance men had taken from the Germans. Others, although they were warned not to, immediately set off to town to loot anything they could get. By nightfall, some had come back with bags full of silver, swords, knives, pistols, watches, clocks, cameras, and anything that looked at all valuable to take home. What Bad Orb didn't experience during the war, it experienced in one day.

We were promised American rations that afternoon, but they never came, and we were fed double rations of the same food that the Germans were feeding us. When there was no pros-pect of getting any American food that afternoon, Charron and I decided to go to town to try and get some. It was dusk already and we had walked about halfway down the road, when we were met by a truck that was taking some men back to camp. "Better not go down there," advised the driver. "It's getting dark and there's a curfew on. They've been giving orders to shoot anybody on the street. Better hop on the back and go back with the rest."

Reluctantly we agreed. We jumped on and sat down between a couple of cases. While riding back, I noticed some of the boys digging into one case and coming up with cigarettes and razor blades. I stuck my hand in, too, and pulled out a carton of Raleighs, while Charron pulled out some Luckies. We slipped these under our shirts. Then I noticed that the case next to me was marked "C Rations." Charron and I both looked at each other. We weren't the only one with the same idea.

When we arrived back at the camp, everybody piled out. Carefully, we threw the box out of the truck, before the driver knew what was going on, and slipped away with it. We decided to share the contents three ways; another fellow would share his third with his friends, and Charron and I would share ours with the boys. We gave Griffin a few rations to share with his buddies and the rest we shared with Brummer, Hammond, Durbin, and Yuskie. We also shared the cigarettes. That night we ate like kings and decided that we were't going to sleep at all. We talked for most of the night with everyone yelling for us to shut up. Finally, at about 5:00 A.M. we dropped off to sleep.

The next day, some BTO (big time operator) went down to Bad Orb again and came back with white bread, cans of bacon, real butter, and gallon cans of stew. They weren't planning to give it away, however, they were selling it for packs of cigarettes. They were looking forward to the day they might get to Paris and sell those cigarettes for two or three hundred francs. We bought some bacon and potatoes and had a feast of French fries.

That evening the C rations promised by the Americans finally arrived. They were a new type of C rations, which we had not seen before. Normally they were despised, but these were different, and, frankly, delicious. Instead of the usual beans and stew, there was a newer and larger variety of meals, including chicken noodles, frankfurters and beans, frankfurter and lima beans, spaghetti and meat balls, and potatoes and eggs. My first can was spaghetti and meat balls. It was a real treat eating my favorite meal again.

On April 4th, facilities were set up to start moving the men out, a certain number each day from each barrack, on a fifty-fifty basis with the Americans and the other nationalities we had in the camp. Most of us wanted to get out as soon as we could, though we didn't mind waiting for a few days. By now, they were feeding us so much that we didn't know what to do with all the food. We had C rations for breakfast, lunch, and supper. At lunch they also gave out some German black bread. The first time I ate it all up, but the next time I threw it away; I had quickly lost my taste for that bread.

Turongian kept buying up food and eating like a horse. He had also bought some potatoes, which he kept in his helmet and secured under his arm wherever he went, afraid that someone might steal them. He would stand there in his long overcoat, the potatoes under his arm, his gaunt figure back-lighted by the falling sun, and with his beard, he was the very image of a devil waiting for someone to make a play for his treasure. One day, he ate so much that he paced the floor and moaned all night. I had some trouble the next night. I couldn't sit, I couldn't lie down, I couldn't stand up. It was a bad thing to feed us so much so soon, and let us eat what we wanted. Our stomachs had shrunk during the three and a half months we had been there and couldn't stand the strain that we were giving it now. The toilet holes were filled to the brim every night and every corner in that room began to pile up debris.

Among the first to be taken out of the camp were the boys in the hospital, of which we had a few. Some had contracted meningitis toward the end of our stay, and our medics and German doctors (there may have been a total of two) did their best to take care of them. At least one fellow didn't make it, dying two days before we were liberated.

Due to an error on the part of Warren, our barrack was one of the last ones scheduled to be evacuated. After the fifth day, everybody was beginning to complain. "The hell with the British," someone moaned. "Let's get the Americans out first." When they learned that the hospital was shipping out all men who claimed to have stomach problems, half the barrack took off for the hospital. We decided to wait so that we could be shipped back together.

There wasn't much to do while we waited to get moved out, though they tried to keep us occupied. One day I went to the movies which was being shown in the Stamlager headquarters, my first one in over four months. It was *Rhapsody in Blue,* which I enjoyed very much, despite its length, especially for its music. (Sitting through the two-hour-and-twenty-minute show, however, was very uncomfortable. I had lost 45 pounds—I weighed 160 pounds when I was captured—and I was sitting on bones rather than meat). On the way back, I met Charron, who wanted to go to Bad Orb to see what we could pick up. I decided against it and we both went back to the barrack.

"Hammond took off," said Charron.

"I thought he wanted us to stick together," I said. Charron merely grunted.

As we reached the barrack, we met Turongian and Brummer, who were hurrying their way to the hospital.

"We're going to the hospital," one of them said. "C'mon let's go."

"Take off," I said, and waved them on.

We walked in the barrack and were surprised to see Durbin and Yuskie still there.

"How come you didn't go with the boys?" I asked.

"We said we'd go back together, didn't we?" answered Durbin.

Charron and I looked at each other.

"Yeah," I replied, "but it looks like somebody forgot."

We waited another three days before they got around to us and finally, on April 11th, they put us on trucks and we said our last good-byes to Bad Orb. We were heading for a delousing station, where we were given a thorough delousing, hot showers, and a complete new outfit. Then we climbed aboard another truck, which took us to an airfield. A half-hour later, we were aboard a C-47 and on our way to Le Havre. This was my first plane ride, and I enjoyed it without getting sick. I realized then that my vertigo had nothing to do with my equilibrium when confined, as in a room or in an airplane. Maybe I should have tried harder when I applied for the Air Force while at Camp Upton, but where would I be now? Instead, I reveled in the ride. I especially enjoyed looking down on the terrain below and seeing the mess that each city and town had been reduced to. We arrived at an airfield near Le Havre at about 4:30 that afternoon. There we boarded another truck that took us to a camp about forty miles away. Camp Lucky Strike, also known as RAMP (Repatriate All Military Personnel) Camp.

The first thing we did there after being assigned to a tent was to have dinner. And what a dinner it was! White bread, fresh meat, and fresh fruit, oranges that I hadn't tasted in months. There was an enormous line, and we waited again for seconds and stuffed ourselves until we thought we would burst.

The next day, I went to a dentist. I had developed trench mouth toward the end of our stay at the Stamlager, and I was looking for some relief. He was a young dentist, about twenty-four years of age. He sat me down, looked at my teeth and asked me my age. I told him that I was nineteen.

"Well," he said, "by the time you're twenty-one you won't have a tooth in your mouth." He prescribed peroxide, the same thing that I was taking at the Stamlager. I walked out of his tent without thanking him. He was wrong, of course, and I wasn't to lose my first tooth until ten years later.

Life at Camp Lucky Strike was fairly pleasant. We had most of the time to ourselves, and while we waited for the next boat to be available, we did almost nothing but eat and go to the movies. Mostly, however, it was eating. When we weren't eating in the mess halls, we were drinking eggnogs at the tents (which were given between meals) eating oranges, or going to the Red Cross for donuts and coffee. Apparently there were others who were doing that, and more, too. Warren, who had been shipped out of Bad Orb as an emergency case when he ate so much that they thought he had appendicitis, recovered from that only to go again and eat half a chicken, with dire results. He died, a rather sad and ironic ending for him. Another fellow ate thirty-three donuts at one sitting and didn't fare well either, as he met the same end. Otherwise, everyone was waiting around like a lot of pregnant women. It looked comical. Anyone you'd ever meet in the camp looked at you and slapped his stomach.

On April 20th or thereabouts (I do not have a record of the exact date), we boarded a ship headed for New York. We were part of a convoy, this time, as opposed to the *Queen Elizabeth*'s or the *Aquitania*'s zigzag east. As a result, it took us about two weeks to get home. Meanwhile, I started to gather these notes together and put them in some logical sequence. Much of this writing was done on the boat.

On May 6th, we arrived in New York. On May 8th, sometime in the early afternoon, I found myself walking down 92nd Street toward my house on First Avenue. I greeted some friends who were waiting for me on the stoop, including Mrs. Walsh the superintendent, who gave me a big fat kiss, and I went up one flight to where my parents were waiting for me. I embraced my mother and father and sister—there were some relatives too.

I had made it home again.

*   *   *

My experiences as a prisoner of war in Germany are certainly not unique. After all, the Germans had captured more than 7,000 of us from the 106th Division alone during the Battle of the Bulge. Many of them had even worse experiences marching from west to east and east to west as both the Allies and the Russians closed the vise on the Germans. Certainly, there were many other experiences within a lot longer incarcerations.

Nor do I think it was typical of what many experienced as a result of the Battle of the Bulge. After all, we didn't have to go on work detail, as many did, and we were liberated at least a month sooner than most; we were among the first to be liberated, in fact. But it was typical of the horror, the fears, the bravery, and the floundering in those brief moments of battle; the abject conditions that befell us once we were captured; the monotonous distaste of the unpalatable food as well as the borderline calories for life they afforded; the squalid conditions that forced us to live (and act) like animals. This may be nothing new, but it was an experience that sixty years later remains vivid in the minds of those who participated.

There are a few open items, which I would like to close before I put this typewriter away. To those of us who swore to get together after the war, I don't imagine anyone did. I imagine that several of us wanted to, but none of us ever took the initiative to get the guys together. At least, I didn't, and I didn't get any invitations either. The closest we got to getting together were the annual conventions that were held at various places. I went to the first one, in Indianapolis, but I can't recall meeting anyone there from D Company. (I remember Joe E. Brown was there. He was a regular whenever veterans got together, ever since he lost his son in the war.) As for the many cakes and pies that we had so diligently made in our minds, and so carefully written down on shreds of paper, I admit that I didn't try one of these.

I saw a few people in pictures in the newspapers. The *New York Times* (or *Journal*) carried a picture of Carl Grube when his boat docked in New York. But it was just a picture (great to see him!) but nothing of his experiences. There was a picture (and article) of Victor Moore's son, PFC Robert E. Moore, who was wearing a nice smile even though he lost half his weight in Stamlager IXB. He weighed 120 lbs. when captured, 60 when liberated.

I received a letter (April 4, 1946) from Charley Smith, our mess sergeant. Among other things, he noted that his feet gave him trouble in winter. He also noted that I was writing about my days as a POW and asked me to send him a copy, and that he wouldn't do anything about what I may say about the "mess sergeants and slow burners." (Don't worry, Smitty; I had nothing but the best to say about the "mess," and meant every word of it!)

Of JT, the last time I saw him was in the Stamlager, trading his shoes with the Russians, leaving him with just galoshes. It was near the end of our stay there, and I imagine he survived, cold feet and all. We had little contact in the prison camp, and I know little of his activities there. I imagine he was one of the first ones out; JT was not the type to linger.

With the exception of three fellows, I never did see my buddies again. I've already mentioned Norman Martin, whom I met on Eisenhower Day at the Polo Grounds. He was shattered, and described what happened to some of the boys on that ill-fated march into Germany. Then, sometime later, I saw a fellow coming out of church. It was Tom Visocki, staff sergeant of the first two squads of the company. I was glad to see him, and we spent some time talking about our experiences. Later, I would see him around town (his son leased the Gulf Oil Station nearby.) Visocki recently passed away from a heart attack.

The other fellow was Bob Walker, #15361182. After several attempts over several months, I found him alive and well and biding his time with a replacement processing regiment at Camp Pickett, Virginia. What had happened to him is best told in his own words written in a letter he wrote me in late 1945:

We were captured on December 21. As long as I live I don't think that I could forget that day. After ten days of walking and riding in boxcars we ended up in (Stamlager) IV-B at Muhlberg. I was in the same barracks with Barnes, Darby and Sandviet. Glen (Barnes) and Art (Sandviet) moved out to a noncoms camp. When I left, Darby was still there. They sent a hundred of us out to a work commando in Chemnitz. While there, we had to sweat out bombings and strafing. They tried to work the hell out of us. However, we were so weak that we weren't able to do anything. I escaped twice while I was there. I was caught the first time and put on bread and water for seven days. The other fellows were't getting much more than that. The second time was on May the 8th. I made it to the front lines that time and was liberated. Out of those hundred guys I didn't know a damn soul. I lost 50 lbs while all this was taking place. I have been thinking about that furlough that we had in England. We were lucky.

My brother is okay. He was sent to the Philipines this Summer. He doesn't like that at all. . . .

The fellows at Muhlberg must have had a rougher time than we did. I had lost only 45 pounds; there must be some fascinating stories there. I visited Bob once coming home from Indianapolis.

You would think that the passion for cigarettes in the prison camp would convince a nonsmoker not to smoke. No way! About three weeks after I was home and having nothing to do (we were given a sixty-day furlough, plus ten days in Lake Placid, plus any job that we wanted in the Army), I started to smoke. I wondered what I would have done if I had smoked while we were in the prison camp. Possibly nothing, as I was determined to quit "cold turkey," which is what I did, thirty-three years later.

Finally, I would like to summarize a few dates that were pertinent to our experience:

December 8, 1943: I arrived at Camp Upton, NY. One year later, (1944) the 106th moved up to the front; and got there Dec. 11th.

December 16, 1944: The beginning of the Battle of the Bulge.

December 19, 1944: Captured.

December 25, 1944: Christmas Day; we arrive at Stamlager IX B.

April 1, 1945: Easter Sunday; Liberated!

May 8, 1945: VE Day. I get home.

It is pertinent also that from December 16 when the Bulge began, up through the last full day we were held captive, we had 106 days of incarceration. Coincident, of course, for the 106th Division, but pertinent nevertheless.

I spoke with my mother about my days as a POW and asked her when she learned that I had been captured. She told me that it was soon after the Battle of the Bulge occurred, and long before she heard from either me or the War Department. She kept calling for me and kept asking for a sign. (She believed strongly in dreams). Suddenly, in the midst of a bunch of soldiers, I presented myself, smiled, and disappeared. That convinced my mother that I was alive and that I was a prisoner of war. I asked her to describe the environment. She went on to describe what was, in effect, Gerolstein, with its high cliff in the background. I was amazed. It was then that I realized that there was someone watching over me, and that I had really nothing to worry about. It was a little late, but no less comforting.

Two views of the barracks known as Stamlager IX B, Bad Orb, Germany.

The Headquarters Building, Bad Orb, Germany.

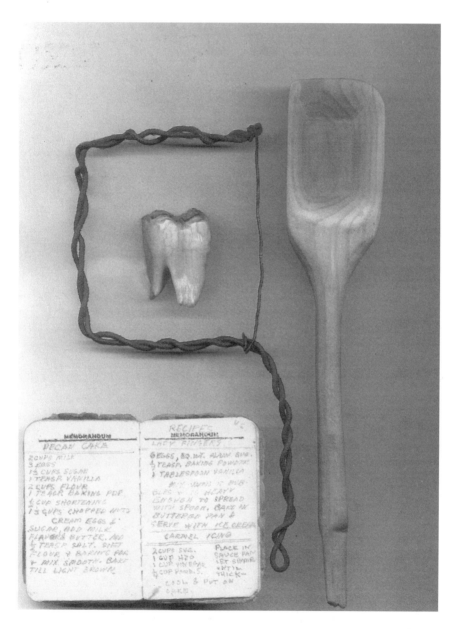

Author's carefully carved spoon, butter/cheese knife, "animal" tooth, and address book containing the many menus concocted.

A picture of the author's medals: the Good Conduct Medal, the Infantry Combat Badge, the Prisoner of War Medal and the Bronze Star Medal.

Post POW at Coney Island, circa 1945: the author with boyhood friends, William Ehni and Horace Kroll.